THE ROYAL LINE OF SUCCESSION

HUGO VICKERS

ROYAL COLLECTION PUBLICATIONS

Published by
Royal Collection Enterprises Ltd
St James's Palace
London SW1A 1JR

For a complete catalogue of current publications, please write to the address above, or visit our website at www.royalcollection.org.uk

010239

ISBN 978 1 902163 39 0
British Library Cataloguing in Publication Data:
A catalogue record of this book is available from the British Library.

Designed by Baseline Arts Ltd, Oxford
Production by Debbie Wayment
Printed and bound by Norwich Colour Print Ltd

For tickets and booking information on visiting Windsor Castle, Buckingham Palace, or the Palace of Holyroodhouse, or for tickets and exhibition information on The Queen's Galleries at either Buckingham Palace or Holyroodhouse, please contact:

Ticket Sales and Information Office
Buckingham Palace
London SW1A 1AA

Booking line: +44 (0)20 7766 7300
Group bookings: +44 (0)20 7766 7321
Fax: +44 (0)20 7930 9625
Email: bookinginfo@royalcollection.org.uk
groupbookings@royalcollection.org.uk
www.royalcollection.org.uk

FRONTISPIECE: *The Family of George III*, 1782–3, Thomas Gainsborough. Gainsborough shows George III and Queen Charlotte at top left, and thirteen of their children in order of birth. The King and Queen had fifteen children in all.

RIGHT: The Royal Arms (see inside front cover).

CONTENTS

This book shows the royal line of succession. Sons take precedence over daughters in the order of succession, so they have been listed first in the main genealogical family trees, regardless of actual order of birth.

INTRODUCTION

THE UNITED KINGDOM HAS A HEREDITARY MONARCHY, whereby the Crown passes by succession from one monarch to another. This system is based on the rules of the inheritance of land, and on primogeniture, according to which if there is a direct male heir, he takes precedence over the females of the family. If the Sovereign has a daughter but no son, she takes precedence over the other male members of the family. Thus Queen Elizabeth II succeeded to the throne because her father, King George VI, had no son and she was his elder daughter.

Fitness to rule was also a consideration from the earliest days of the English monarchy, when the reigning king often bypassed his immediate successor in favour of a more suitable candidate who could provide leadership. This was sometimes unpopular, and fierce battles were frequently fought by rival contenders. There are two other elements that have been incorporated over the centuries: the **statutory principle** and the **elective principle**. The element of statute was established in the Bill of Rights of 1689, allowing Parliament to regulate the succession to the throne, and was strengthened by the Act of Settlement in 1701 (for details of both see page 64), which permitted Parliament to determine the title to the throne. The British monarchy today is thus properly described as both hereditary and constitutional.

Subject to the Bill of Rights, a new sovereign succeeds to the throne automatically, but has some obligations, normally attending the first opening of Parliament of the reign and at that ceremony promising to go to Westminster Abbey for the Coronation. The Sovereign will not be anointed and crowned and thus acknowledged as king or queen unless he or she takes the Coronation Oath.

The Act of Settlement ensured that a Roman Catholic could not become Sovereign, nor could the Sovereign be married to a Roman Catholic. The Sovereign is obliged to be in communion with the Church of England, and to preserve the established Church of England and the established Church of Scotland. In the accession declaration, he or she must promise to uphold the Protestant succession.

The royal line of succession is now well established, and the constitutional machinery is well in place, but it was not always so. The family trees in this book trace 2,000 years of the sometimes troubled histories of the men and women who, by accident of birth, found themselves in line to reign.

Henry VIII, Henry VII, Elizabeth of York and Jane Seymour, copy by Remigius Van Leemput, 1667, of Holbein's original of 1537.

1537
SI IVVAT HEROVM CLARAS VIDISSE FIGVRAS,
SPECTA HAS, MAIORES NVLLA TABELLA TVLIT.
CERTAMEN MAGNVM, LIS, QVÆSTIO MAGNA PATERNE,
FILIVS AN VINCAT. VICIT. VTERQVE QVIDEM.
ISTE SVOS HOSTES, PATRIÆQVE INCENDIA SÆPE
SVSTVLIT, ET PACEM CIVIBVS VSQVE DEDIT.
FILIVS AD MAIORA QVIDEM PROGNATVS AB ARIS
SVBMOVET INDIGNOS ET SVBSTITVITQVE PROBOS.
CERTÆ, VIRTVTI, PAPARVM AVDACIA CESSIT,
HENRICO OCTAVO SCEPTRA GERENTE MANV
REDDITA RELIGIO EST, ISTO REGNANTE DEIQVE
DOGMATA CEPERVNT ESSE IN HONORE SVO.
PROTOTYPVM IVSTÆ MAGNITVDINIS IPSO OPERE TECTORIO
FECIT HOLBENIVS IVBENTE HENRICO VIII.
ECTYPVM A REMIGIO VAN LEEMPVT BREVIORI TABELLA
DESCRIBI VOLVIT CAROLVS II. M. B. F. E. H. R.
A°. DNI. MDCLXVII.

PRE-CONQUEST KINGS

THERE ARE SAID TO HAVE BEEN TWENTY-FOUR GENERATIONS OF SAXON CHIEFTAINS PRECEDING CERDIC, KING OF WESSEX (r.519–34), THE SAXON INVADER WHO REPUTEDLY FOUNDED HIS OWN KINGDOM AFTER ARRIVING IN ENGLAND IN 495. THESE GENEALOGIES, WHICH MAY HAVE SOME ACCURACY, WERE PASSED DOWN ORALLY AND EVENTUALLY LISTED IN THE 9TH-CENTURY *ANGLO-SAXON CHRONICLE*. SUCCESSORS TO CERDIC RULED NOT ONLY BY DESCENT; THE EARLY KINGS OF WESSEX ALSO HAD TO PROVE THEIR FITNESS TO RULE.

By AD 650, the British Isles comprised a number of territories, some ruled by native kings, some ruled by the immigrant Angles, Saxons and Jutes who had invaded southern Britain during the 5th century. It was a period of great struggle for survival, as well as for supremacy. In essence, these rulers were tribal chieftains, whom later Latin writers described as *reges* or kings.

Their kingdoms came to be known as 'the Heptarchy' or the rule of seven: Bernicia and Deira (which joined together to create Northumbria in AD 651), Lindsey, East Anglia, Mercia, Wessex and Kent. These evolved into Northumbria, Essex, East Anglia, Mercia, Wessex, Sussex and Kent, and the lineage of Cerdic of Wessex is most often credited with having laid the foundations of the British monarchy.

The Venerable Bede (672–735), who chronicled the early history of England in his *Ecclesiastical History of the English People*, identified a further seven warrior kings as important figures. Of these, Ceawlin (r.560–91) and Ine (r.688–726) were of particular importance. Cynegils (r.611–43) was one of the first kings to embrace the Christian faith; while both Caedwalla (r.685–8) and Ine abdicated in order to make pilgrimages to Rome.

In the 9th century Egbert, King of Wessex (r.802–39), founded a united England by subduing the various other kingdoms, and was pronounced 'King of the English'. However, it was during this period that Britain faced a series of invasions from Denmark, and the prospect of Viking kings on the English throne.

The line of succession overleaf shows the Kings of All England from Egbert to Edward the Confessor (r.1042–66).

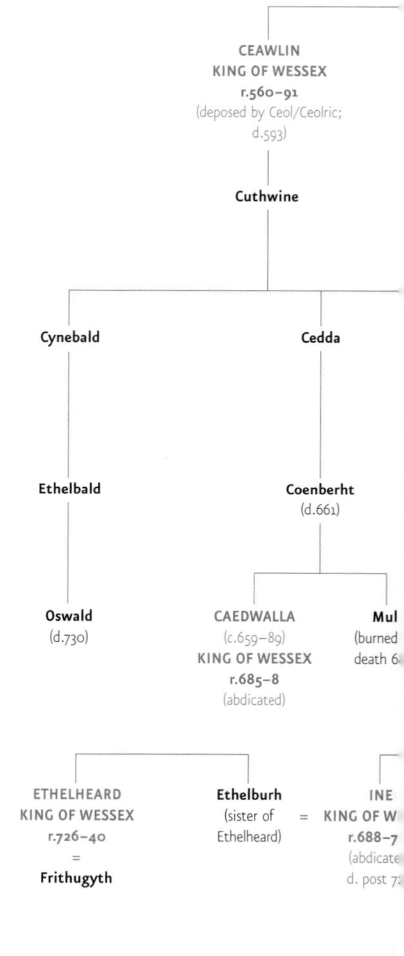

b. – born	div. – divorced	= – married
c. – *circa* (about)	k. – killed	≠ – not married
d. – died	m. – marriage	
diss. – dissolved	r. – reigned	

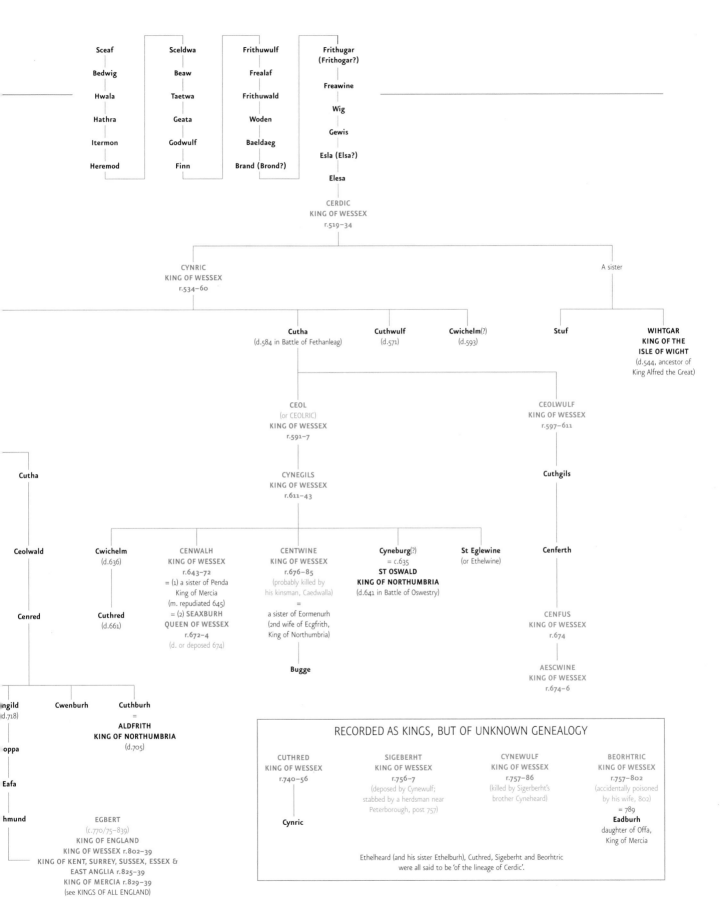

Sceaf
Bedwig
Hwala
Hathra
Itermon
Heremod

Sceldwa
Beaw
Taetwa
Geata
Godwulf
Finn

Frithuwulf
Frealaf
Frithuwald
Woden
Baeldaeg
Brand (Brond?)

Frithugar (Frithogar?)
Freawine
Wig
Gewis
Esla (Elsa?)
Elesa

CERDIC
KING OF WESSEX
r.519–34

CYNRIC
KING OF WESSEX
r.534–60

A sister

Cutha
(d.584 in Battle of Fethanleag)

Cuthwulf
(d.571)

Cwichelm(?)
(d.593)

Stuf

WIHTGAR
KING OF THE ISLE OF WIGHT
(d.544, ancestor of King Alfred the Great)

CEOL
(or CEOLRIC)
KING OF WESSEX
r.591–7

CEOLWULF
KING OF WESSEX
r.597–611

Cutha

CYNEGILS
KING OF WESSEX
r.611–43

Cuthgils

Ceolwald

Cwichelm
(d.636)

CENWALH
KING OF WESSEX
r.643–72
= (1) a sister of Penda King of Mercia
(m. repudiated 645)
= (2) SEAXBURH
QUEEN OF WESSEX
r.672–4
(d. or deposed 674)

CENTWINE
KING OF WESSEX
r.676–85
(probably killed by his kinsman, Caedwalla)
=
a sister of Eormenurh
(2nd wife of Ecgfrith, King of Northumbria)

Cyneburg(?)
= c.635
ST OSWALD
KING OF NORTHUMBRIA
(d.641 in Battle of Oswestry)

St Eglewine
(or Ethelwine)

Cenferth

Cenred

Cuthred
(d.661)

Bugge

CENFUS
KING OF WESSEX
r.674

AESCWINE
KING OF WESSEX
r.674–6

ngild
d.718)

Cwenburh

Cuthburh
=
ALDFRITH
KING OF NORTHUMBRIA
(d.705)

oppa

Eafa

hmund

EGBERT
(c.770/75–839)
KING OF ENGLAND
KING OF WESSEX r.802–39
KING OF KENT, SURREY, SUSSEX, ESSEX & EAST ANGLIA r.825–39
KING OF MERCIA r.829–39
(see KINGS OF ALL ENGLAND)

RECORDED AS KINGS, BUT OF UNKNOWN GENEALOGY

CUTHRED
KING OF WESSEX
r.740–56

Cynric

SIGEBERHT
KING OF WESSEX
r.756–7
(deposed by Cynewulf; stabbed by a herdsman near Peterborough, post 757)

CYNEWULF
KING OF WESSEX
r.757–86
(killed by Sigerberht's brother Cyneheard)

BEORHTRIC
KING OF WESSEX
r.757–802
(accidentally poisoned by his wife, 802)
= 789
Eadburh
daughter of Offa, King of Mercia

Ethelheard (and his sister Ethelburh), Cuthred, Sigeberht and Beorhtric were all said to be 'of the lineage of Cerdic'.

Kings of All England

EGBERT
(c.770/75–839)
KING OF ENGLAND
KING OF WESSEX r.802–39
KING OF KENT, SURREY, SUSSEX, ESSEX & EAST ANGLIA r.825–3
KING OF MERCIA r.829–39

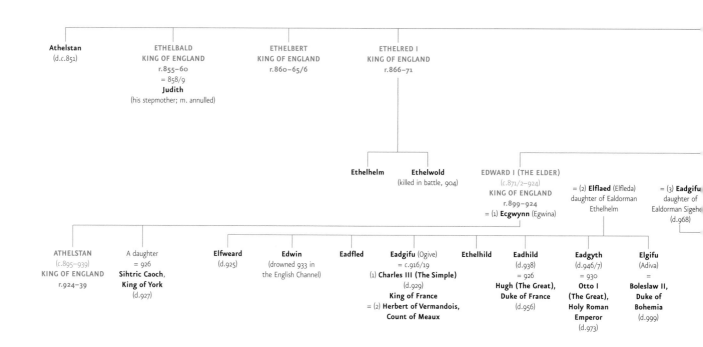

Athelstan
(d.c.851)

ETHELBALD
KING OF ENGLAND
r.855–60
= 858/9
Judith
(his stepmother; m. annulled)

ETHELBERT
KING OF ENGLAND
r.860–65/6

ETHELRED I
KING OF ENGLAND
r.866–71

Ethelhelm

Ethelwold
(killed in battle, 904)

EDWARD I (THE ELDER)
(c.871/2–924)
KING OF ENGLAND
r.899–924
= (1) **Ecgwynn** (Egwina)
= (2) **Elflaed** (Elfleda)
daughter of Ealdorman Ethelhelm
= (3) **Eadgifu**
daughter of Ealdorman Sigehe
(d.968)

ATHELSTAN
(c.895–939)
KING OF ENGLAND
r.924–39

A daughter
= 926
Sihtric Caoch, King of York
(d.927)

Elfweard
(d.925)

Edwin
(drowned 933 in the English Channel)

Eadfled

Eadgifu (Ogive)
= c.916/19
(1) **Charles III (The Simple)**
(d.929)
King of France
= (2) **Herbert of Vermandois, Count of Meaux**

Ethelhild

Eadhild
(d.938)
= 926
Hugh (The Great), Duke of France
(d.956)

Eadgyth
(d.946/7)
= 930
Otto I (The Great), Holy Roman Emperor
(d.973)

Elgifu
(Adiva)
=
Boleslaw II, Duke of Bohemia
(d.999)

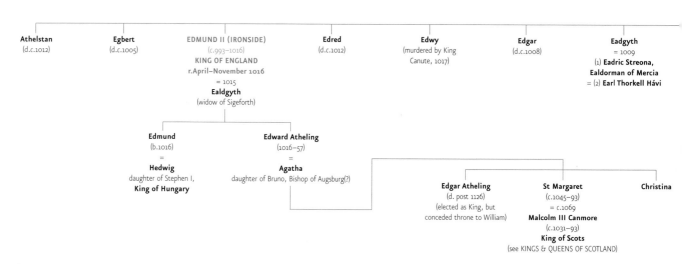

Athelstan
(d.c.1012)

Egbert
(d.c.1005)

EDMUND II (IRONSIDE)
(c.993–1016)
KING OF ENGLAND
r.April–November 1016
= 1015
Ealdgyth
(widow of Sigeforth)

Edred
(d.c.1012)

Edwy
(murdered by King Canute, 1017)

Edgar
(d.c.1008)

Eadgyth
= 1009
(1) **Eadric Streona, Ealdorman of Mercia**
= (2) **Earl Thorkell Hávi**

Edmund
(b.1016)
=
Hedwig
daughter of Stephen I,
King of Hungary

Edward Atheling
(1016–57)
=
Agatha
daughter of Bruno, Bishop of Augsburg(?)

Edgar Atheling
(d. post 1126)
(elected as King, but conceded throne to William)

St Margaret
(c.1045–93)
= c.1069
Malcolm III Canmore
(c.1031–93)
King of Scots
(see KINGS & QUEENS OF SCOTLAND)

Christina

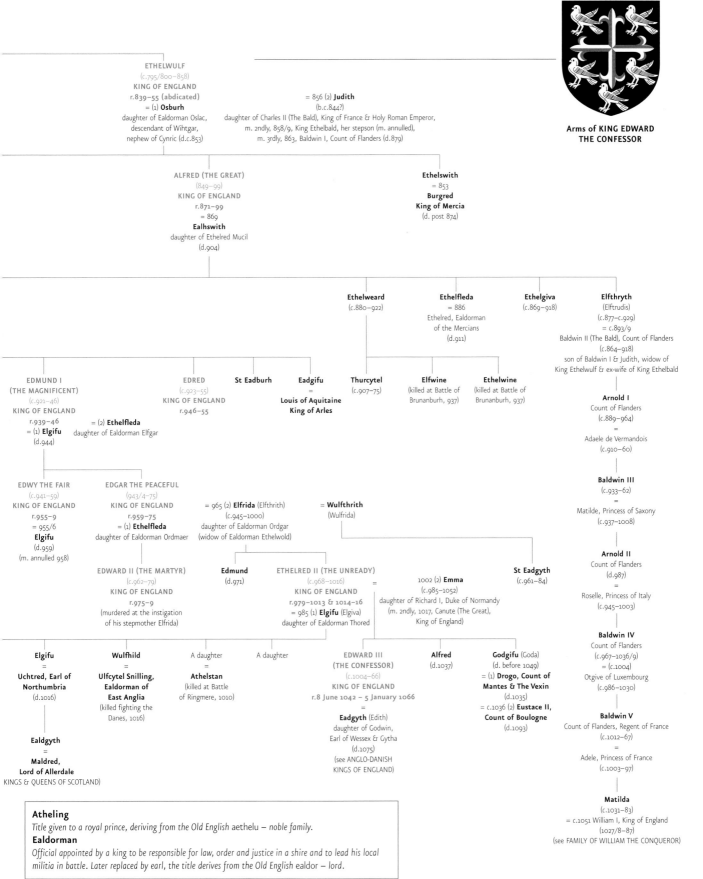

Arms of KING EDWARD THE CONFESSOR

ETHELWULF
(c.795/800–858)
KING OF ENGLAND
r.839–55 (abdicated)
= (1) **Osburh**
daughter of Ealdorman Oslac,
descendant of Wihtgar,
nephew of Cynric (d.c.853)

= 856 (2) **Judith**
(b.c.844?)
daughter of Charles II (The Bald), King of France & Holy Roman Emperor,
m. 2ndly, 858/9, King Ethelbald, her stepson (m. annulled),
m. 3rdly, 863, Baldwin I, Count of Flanders (d.879)

ALFRED (THE GREAT)
(849–99)
KING OF ENGLAND
r.871–99
= 869
Ealhswith
daughter of Ethelred Mucil
(d.904)

Ethelswith
= 853
Burgred
King of Mercia
(d. post 874)

Ethelweard
(c.880–922)

Ethelfleda
= 886
Ethelred, Ealdorman
of the Mercians
(d.911)

Ethelgiva
(c.869–918)

Elfthryth
(Elftrudis)
(c.877–c.929)
= c.893/9
Baldwin II (The Bald), Count of Flanders
(c.864–918)
son of Baldwin I & Judith, widow of
King Ethelwulf & ex-wife of King Ethelbald

EDMUND I
(THE MAGNIFICENT)
(c.921–46)
KING OF ENGLAND
r.939–46
= (1) **Elgifu**
(d.944)
= (2) **Ethelfleda**
daughter of Ealdorman Elfgar

EDRED
(c.923–55)
KING OF ENGLAND
r.946–55

St Eadburh

Eadgifu
=
Louis of Aquitaine
King of Arles

Thurcytel
(c.907–75)

Elfwine
(killed at Battle of
Brunanburh, 937)

Ethelwine
(killed at Battle of
Brunanburh, 937)

Arnold I
Count of Flanders
(c.889–964)
=
Adaele de Vermandois
(c.910–60)

EDWY THE FAIR
(c.941–59)
KING OF ENGLAND
r.955–9
= 955/6
Elgifu
(d.959)
(m. annulled 958)

EDGAR THE PEACEFUL
(943/4–75)
KING OF ENGLAND
r.959–75
= (1) **Ethelfleda**
daughter of Ealdorman Ordmaer

= 965 (2) **Elfrida** (Elfthrith)
(c.945–1000)
daughter of Ealdorman Ordgar
(widow of Ealdorman Ethelwold)

= **Wulfthrith**
(Wulfrida)

Baldwin III
(c.933–62)
=
Matilde, Princess of Saxony
(c.937–1008)

EDWARD II (THE MARTYR)
(c.962–79)
KING OF ENGLAND
r.975–9
(murdered at the instigation
of his stepmother Elfrida)

Edmund
(d.971)

ETHELRED II (THE UNREADY)
(c.968–1016)
KING OF ENGLAND
r.979–1013 & 1014–16
= 985 (1) **Elgifu** (Elgiva)
daughter of Ealdorman Thored

= 1002 (2) **Emma**
(c.985–1052)
daughter of Richard I, Duke of Normandy
(m. 2ndly, 1017, Canute (The Great),
King of England)

St Eadgyth
(c.961–84)

Arnold II
Count of Flanders
(d.987)
=
Roselle, Princess of Italy
(c.945–1003)

Elgifu
=
Uchtred, Earl of Northumbria
(d.1016)

Ealdgyth
=
Maldred,
Lord of Allerdale
KINGS & QUEENS OF SCOTLAND)

Wulfhild
=
Ulfcytel Snilling,
Ealdorman of
East Anglia
(killed fighting the
Danes, 1016)

A daughter
=
Athelstan
(killed at Battle
of Ringmere, 1010)

A daughter

EDWARD III
(THE CONFESSOR)
(c.1004–66)
KING OF ENGLAND
r.8 June 1042 – 5 January 1066
=
Eadgyth (Edith)
daughter of Godwin,
Earl of Wessex & Gytha
(d.1075)
(see ANGLO-DANISH
KINGS OF ENGLAND)

Alfred
(d.1037)

Godgifu (Goda)
(d. before 1049)
= (1) **Drogo, Count of**
Mantes & The Vexin
(d.1035)
= c.1036 (2) **Eustace II,**
Count of Boulogne
(d.1093)

Baldwin IV
Count of Flanders
(c.967–1036/9)
= (c.1004)
Otgive of Luxembourg
(c.986–1030)

Baldwin V
Count of Flanders, Regent of France
(c.1012–67)
=
Adele, Princess of France
(c.1003–97)

Matilda
(c.1031–83)
= c.1051 William I, King of England
(1027/8–87)
(see FAMILY OF WILLIAM THE CONQUEROR)

Atheling
Title given to a royal prince, deriving from the Old English aethelu – noble family.
Ealdorman
Official appointed by a king to be responsible for law, order and justice in a shire and to lead his local militia in battle. Later replaced by earl, the title derives from the Old English ealdor – lord.

Around 799, Egbert had been driven into exile by Beorhtric, the then King of Wessex. Egbert returned to England as King of the West Saxons, and in 802 subdued Cornwall, defeated the King of Mercia and annexed Kent, becoming overlord of all the English kings in 829.

On his death in 839 Egbert was succeeded by his son Ethelwulf. Most of Ethelwulf's reign was spent repelling raids by the Danes. After the death of his first wife, Ethelwulf made a pilgrimage to Rome, and on his return through France he married Judith, daughter of Charles II (The Bald), King of France. This established a strong bond against the Vikings with the most powerful country in Christendom. When Ethelwulf died in 858 his son Ethelbald, king since 855, married his widowed stepmother, perhaps to try to preserve this alliance. After Ethelbald's death, three of his brothers reigned in succession, one of whom, Ethelred I (r.866–71), fought in six battles against the Danes, eventually dying of wounds sustained at the Battle of Merton.

The youngest brother, Alfred, was crowned in 871, and came to be known as Alfred the Great. His reign was also spent fighting the Danes and in 878 he was forced to retreat to Athelney in Somerset where, preoccupied with military strategy, he famously 'burnt the cakes' he had been asked to watch by a herdsman's wife. However, he managed to hold Wessex, took London in 886, and went on to build a large fleet and an army for his kingdom. He imposed a strong sense of regal authority and Christian morality on his people, introduced codes of law and religious and educational reforms, and as a result greatly strengthened the position of the monarchy.

Alfred was succeeded by his son Edward I (the Elder) in 899, though the succession was disputed by Edward's cousin Ethelwold (the son of Ethelred I). Edward subdued the Welsh and ruled as far north as the Humber. His overlordship was recognized by some of the kings of Northumbria and Scotland. He was succeeded in 924 by his son Athelstan, who extended his overlordship even further into the kingdoms of York and Scotland; it is said he never lost a battle. A figure of great eminence, he was respected by foreign kings, bishops and nobles; and

The Bayeux Tapestry (held in Caen, Normandy) has representations of Edward the Confessor, Harold II and William the Conqueror. (LEFT) Edward the Confessor, portrayed as old and wise; (RIGHT) William is reminding Harold of his oath of allegiance.

forged alliances by marrying four of his half-sisters to European rulers.

Athelstan died unmarried in 939 and was succeeded by his half-brother Edmund I who was known as Edmund the Magnificent. Edmund I seized control of many towns from the Danes, including Leicester and Derby. He also forged an alliance with Malcolm I, King of the Scots, by handing over Northumbria and Strathclyde. Edmund was killed in the course of a struggle with an intruder at Pucklechurch, Gloucestershire, in 946 and was succeeded by his brother Edred as his own sons were too young to take the throne.

On Edred's death in 955, Edmund's son Edwy the Fair became King. Edwy's untimely death meant that his brother Edgar the Peaceful succeeded him. Edgar's authority extended to Ireland and his was a largely peaceful reign, during which he helped to establish the English monastic system with Dunstan, Archbishop of Canterbury.

Edward II (the Martyr), the next King, was Edgar's son by his first marriage. His succession to the throne was disputed by his stepmother, Elfrida, who wanted to see her own son, Ethelred, crowned. Edward was murdered on Elfrida's orders while on a hunting trip.

Ethelred II was a mere boy when he became King, earning him the nickname of 'The Unready' or 'The Redeless', since he was deemed unable to discern good *rede* or counsel. He struggled to fend off Danish raids and eventually instituted the Danegeld, a regular payment to buy off the Danes. This was maintained until Ethelred ordered a massacre of all Danes in England in 1003. A period of further attacks and invasions ensued, and Ethelred lost the throne to Sweyn Forkbeard, King of Denmark, in 1013. Ethelred fled to Normandy.

Sweyn was the son of Harold Bluetooth, King of Denmark. He had made various conquests in Sweden and Norway and his raids on Britain began in 991. Having ousted Ethelred in 1013 to become the first Danish King of England, he died the following year. At this point the throne reverted to Ethelred II.

Ethelred's son Edmund II succeeded him in April 1016, reigning until November of that year. He spent his short reign in continual warfare and his bravery earned him the nickname of 'Ironside'. After being defeated by Canute, the son of Sweyn, at Ashington in Essex, Edmund agreed to divide the kingdom with Canute. But Edmund died in 1016, and Canute became sole ruler until his death in 1035.

Canute did not treat England as a conquered country, but divided it into five earldoms or provinces. Although ruthless in the methods used to establish his position (he carried out a series of assassinations to prevent any threat to his succession, and even married as his second wife the widow of Ethelred, to secure his line), he proved to be an exceptionally capable and respected ruler.

Canute was succeeded in 1035 by two sons by his two marriages, who reigned jointly for two years: Harold I (Harefoot) and Hardicanute. Harold, the son of Elfgiva of Northampton, was King of the district north of the Thames. Hardicanute spent most of his time in Denmark, so Harold was made sole King of England in 1037 and reigned until his death in 1040. Hardicanute was sole King from 1040 until his own death in 1042.

During the long conflict with the Danes, the English throne had been twice lost to Danish kings: first to Sweyn and then to Canute. But in 1042 the English royal family was restored with the succession of Edward the Confessor, half-brother of Edmund II and also half-brother of Canute's son, Hardicanute.

In January 1066 Edward, a venerable and deeply pious man, died childless. The Witan (council) elected his brother-in-law, Harold Godwinson – who was the son of the all-powerful Godwin, Earl of Wessex – as King Harold II.

Harold II had to cope with contenders to the throne from all sides. William, Duke of Normandy, declared that Edward the Confessor had promised the crown to him, and that Harold had sworn to aid William's accession to the throne when held captive in Normandy in 1053. A further claim came from the King of Norway. Harold II won a victory over the Norwegians at Stamford Bridge, near York, on 25 September 1066, but was killed in battle against William at Hastings on 14 October.

In 1066, after the death of Harold II, Edgar Atheling, a grandson of Edmund II, was briefly elected King by the English, but conceded the crown to the Norman William the Conqueror. Edgar, the last in the family line of Cerdic, died some time after 1126.

Harald
King of Denmark
r.1014–19

CANUTE (THE GRE
(c.995–1035)
KING OF ENGLAN
r.30 November 101
12 November 103
=
(1) **Elfgiva**
daughter of Aelfhelr
Ealdorman of Northan
(m. repudiated)

Sweyn
(d.1036)
King of Norway

HAROLD I (HAREFC
(c.1016–40)
JOINT KING OF ENG
with his half-brot
Hardicanute
r.1035–7
SOLE KING OF ENGL
r.1037 – 17 March 1

Harold II as depicted in the Bayeux Tapestry at his Coronation in 1066, sceptre and orb in his hands.

Anglo-Danish Kings of England

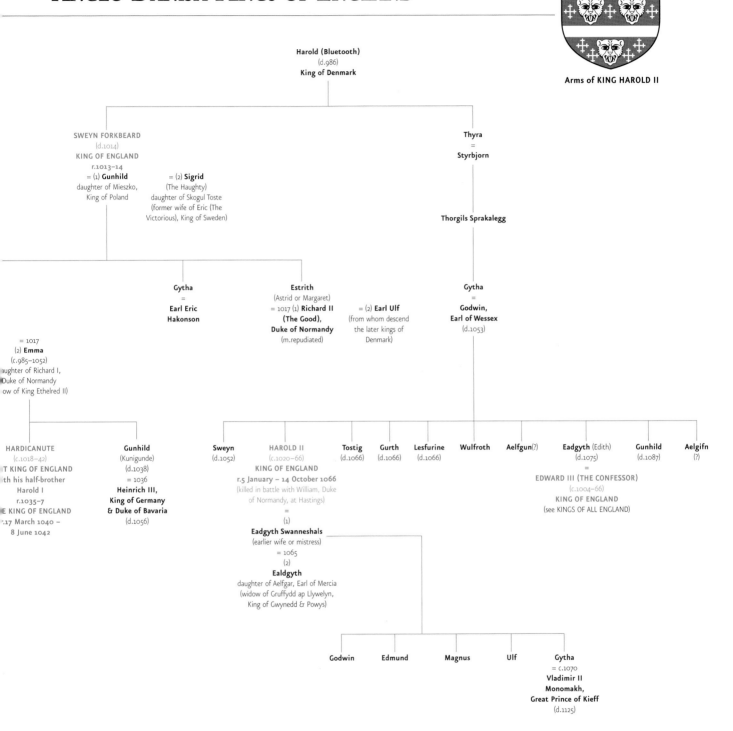

Arms of KING HAROLD II

Harold (Bluetooth)
(d.986)
King of Denmark

SWEYN FORKBEARD
(d.1014)
KING OF ENGLAND
r.1013–14
= (1) **Gunhild**
daughter of Mieszko,
King of Poland

= (2) **Sigrid**
(The Haughty)
daughter of Skogul Toste
(former wife of Eric (The Victorious), King of Sweden)

Thyra
=
Styrbjorn

Thorgils Sprakalegg

Gytha
=
Earl Eric Hakonson

Estrith
(Astrid or Margaret)
= 1017 (1) **Richard II (The Good), Duke of Normandy**
(m.repudiated)

= (2) **Earl Ulf**
(from whom descend the later kings of Denmark)

Gytha
=
Godwin, Earl of Wessex
(d.1053)

= 1017
(2) **Emma**
(c.985–1052)
aughter of Richard I,
Duke of Normandy
ow of King Ethelred II)

HARDICANUTE
(c.1018–42)
T KING OF ENGLAND
th his half-brother
Harold I
r.1035–7
E KING OF ENGLAND
.17 March 1040 –
8 June 1042

Gunhild
(Kunigunde)
(d.1038)
= 1036
Heinrich III, King of Germany & Duke of Bavaria
(d.1056)

Sweyn
(d.1052)

HAROLD II
(c.1020–66)
KING OF ENGLAND
r.5 January – 14 October 1066
(killed in battle with William, Duke of Normandy, at Hastings)
=
(1)
Eadgyth Swanneshals
(earlier wife or mistress)
= 1065
(2)
Ealdgyth
daughter of Aelfgar, Earl of Mercia
(widow of Gruffydd ap Llywelyn, King of Gwynedd & Powys)

Tostig
(d.1066)

Gurth
(d.1066)

Lesfurine
(d.1066)

Wulfroth

Aelfgun(?)

Eadgyth (Edith)
(d.1075)
=
EDWARD III (THE CONFESSOR)
(c.1004–66)
KING OF ENGLAND
(see KINGS OF ALL ENGLAND)

Gunhild
(d.1087)

Aelgifn
(?)

Godwin

Edmund

Magnus

Ulf

Gytha
= c.1070
Vladimir II Monomakh, Great Prince of Kieff
(d.1125)

Family of William the Conqueror

FOLLOWING HIS VICTORY AT THE BATTLE OF HASTINGS, WILLIAM I TOOK THE THRONE OF ENGLAND AND REIGNED FROM 1066 TO 1087. HAVING INVADED ENGLAND AND DEFEATED HAROLD II AT HASTINGS, HE WAS CROWNED AT WESTMINSTER ABBEY ON CHRISTMAS DAY 1066. HE REIGNED WISELY, AND IS CREDITED WITH THE INTRODUCTION OF A SYSTEM OF CENTRALIZED FEUDALISM. HE INSTIGATED A SURVEY OF ENGLAND, KNOWN TO US AS THE DOMESDAY BOOK. HIS WIFE, MATILDA, WAS A DIRECT DESCENDANT OF ALFRED THE GREAT.

William's claim to the throne was derived from personal and political links, and most importantly because in about 1051 Edward the Confessor promised him the succession. He obtained papal approval to invade England, and at Hastings defeated Harold II and seized the crown. His eldest son was Robert, Duke of Normandy, who rebelled against him and wounded him in single combat in 1079. Although they were reconciled, Robert remained a problem for his father and William passed him over in the succession. William's second son, Richard, predeceased him, having been killed while on a hunting trip in the New Forest. William designated his third son, William Rufus, his heir.

Known as 'Rufus' or 'The Red King', William II was his father's favourite son and was crowned in 1087. He proved to be unpopular – especially with the Church, because of his opposition to reform and his appropriation of their revenues for his own use. He never married and was killed in mysterious circumstances while hunting in the New Forest.

William II's younger brother, Henry I (Beauclerc), secured the throne. Henry allied himself in marriage with Matilda, daughter of Malcolm III, King of the Scots, thereby securing the friendship of Scotland. Like his father and his brother before him, Henry had to deal with his troublesome brother Robert when the subjects of Robert's duchy, weary of their ruler's incompetence, asked Henry I to intercede on their behalf. Robert was captured and subsequently died in prison.

The 18th-century engraver George Vertue created a series of historical 'portraits' of kings of England. (LEFT) William I; (TOP) Henry I; (ABOVE) King Stephen.

Henry I reigned for thirty-five years, and was known as 'the lion of justice', and as a good diplomatist. His two sons, William and Richard, were drowned in 1120 while crossing the Channel near Barfleur, Normandy, following which Henry's daughter, Matilda, was declared the heiress presumptive. But on Henry I's death, the crown was claimed by Stephen of Blois, his nephew, despite the fact that he had sworn to help Matilda, the rightful heir, to succeed her father. He had gathered support among the citizens of London, and was crowned in 1135.

Stephen faced a difficult period, quelling insurrections by opponents and warring with the Scots. His cousin Matilda had not given up her claim to the throne, and was set to do battle with Stephen in 1139. In 1141 Stephen was captured, although he was freed by his supporters. Civil wars and the struggle for the throne continued for twelve years. In 1148 Matilda left the country, and in 1153 her son Henry, who had taken her place as claimant to the throne, agreed at the Treaty of Winchester to leave Stephen unmolested as long as he succeeded the King on his death. In 1154 Henry became King, and the royal lineage took another turn as Britain entered the era of the great House of Plantagenet.

Family of William the Conqueror

(see ANGLO-DANISH KINGS OF ENGLAND, page 13)

WILLIAM I
(THE CONQUEROR)
(1027/8–87)
KING OF ENGLAND
r.14 October 1066 – 9 September 1087
illegitimate son of Robert le Diable, Duke of Normandy (Robert I 'The Magnificent'), and Herlève, daughter of 'The Tanner', of Falaise

= c.1051

Matilda
(c.1031–83)
QUEEN MATILDA
daughter of Baldwin V, Count of Flanders, Regent of France
(direct descendant of King Alfred the Great)
(see KINGS OF ALL ENGLAND)

Robert II (Curthose)
Duke of Normandy
(c.1051/4–1134)
= 1100
Sibylla
(d.1103)
daughter of Geoffrey, Count of Conservano

Richard
(c.1055–81)
(killed while hunting in the New Forest)

WILLIAM II
(RUFUS)
(c.1055/60–1100)
KING OF ENGLAND
r.9 September 1087 – 2 August 1100
(killed while hunting in the New Forest)

HENRY I
(HENRY BEAUCLERC)
(1068–1135)
KING OF ENGLAND
r.2 August 1100 – 1 December 1135
= 1100
(1) **Matilda** (Edith)
(1079–1118)
QUEEN MATILDA
daughter of Malcolm III, King of Scots & great-granddaughter of King Edmund II

= 1121 (2) **Adeliza**
(c.1104–51)
QUEEN ADELIZA
daughter of Godfrey I (The Bearded), Duke of Lower Lorraine
(who m. 2ndly, 1138, William d'Aubigny, 1st Earl of Arundel (d.1176))

Children of Robert II (Curthose):

William Clito,
Count of Flanders
(1101–28)
(died of a wound received at St Omer)
= 1123 (1) **Sibylla**
(1112–65)
daughter of Fulk V, Count of Anjou & Maine, and sister of Geoffrey V,
(m. annulled 1124)
(who m. 2ndly, 1134, Thierry of Alsace, Count of Flanders)
= 1128 (2) **Joan**
daughter of Guillaume I, Count of Burgundy
(ex-wife of Louis VI, King of France, and widow of Umberto II, Count of Savoy)

Henry
(b.1102)
(killed while hunting in the New Forest)

Children of Henry I:

William the Atheling,
Duke of Normandy
(1103–20)
(drowned off Barfleur, Normandy)
= 1119
Matilda (Alice)
(1107–54)
daughter of Fulk V, Count of Anjou & Maine, and sister of Geoffrey V

Richard
(d.1120)
(drowned off Barfleur, Normandy)

Matilda
(c.1102–67)
Heiress Presumptive
= 1114
(1) **Heinrich V**
(d.1125)
King of Germany, Holy Roman Emperor
= 1127 (2) **Geoffrey V, Count of Anjou & Maine**
brother of Matilda, Duchess of Normandy
(1113–51)

Children of Matilda and Geoffrey V:

HENRY II
(CURTMANTLE)
(1133–89)
KING OF ENGLAND
(see HOUSE OF PLANTAGENET)

Geoffrey VI Martel,
Count of Nantes
(1134–58)

William
(1136–64)

Arms attributed to KING STEPHEN

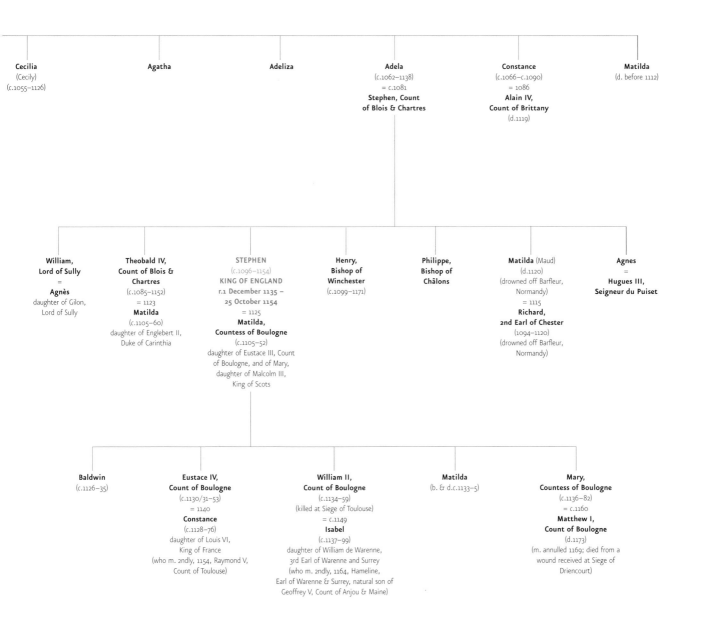

Cecilia
(Cecily)
(c.1055–1126)

Agatha

Adeliza

Adela
(c.1062–1138)
= c.1081
Stephen, Count of Blois & Chartres

Constance
(c.1066–c.1090)
= 1086
Alain IV, Count of Brittany
(d.1119)

Matilda
(d. before 1112)

William, Lord of Sully
=
Agnès
daughter of Gilon, Lord of Sully

Theobald IV, Count of Blois & Chartres
(c.1085–1152)
= 1123
Matilda
(c.1105–60)
daughter of Englebert II, Duke of Carinthia

STEPHEN
(c.1096–1154)
KING OF ENGLAND
r.1 December 1135 – 25 October 1154
= 1125
Matilda, Countess of Boulogne
(c.1105–52)
daughter of Eustace III, Count of Boulogne, and of Mary, daughter of Malcolm III, King of Scots

Henry, Bishop of Winchester
(c.1099–1171)

Philippe, Bishop of Châlons

Matilda (Maud)
(d.1120)
(drowned off Barfleur, Normandy)
= 1115
Richard, 2nd Earl of Chester
(1094–1120)
(drowned off Barfleur, Normandy)

Agnes
=
Hugues III, Seigneur du Puiset

Baldwin
(c.1126–35)

Eustace IV, Count of Boulogne
(c.1130/31–53)
= 1140
Constance
(c.1128–76)
daughter of Louis VI, King of France
(who m. 2ndly, 1154, Raymond V, Count of Toulouse)

William II, Count of Boulogne
(c.1134–59)
(killed at Siege of Toulouse)
= c.1149
Isabel
(c.1137–99)
daughter of William de Warenne, 3rd Earl of Warenne and Surrey
(who m. 2ndly, 1164, Hameline, Earl of Warenne & Surrey, natural son of Geoffrey V, Count of Anjou & Maine)

Matilda
(b. & d.c.1133–5)

Mary, Countess of Boulogne
(c.1136–82)
= c.1160
Matthew I, Count of Boulogne
(d.1173)
(m. annulled 1169; died from a wound received at Siege of Driencourt)

House of Plantagenet

KING HENRY II (CURTMANTLE) WAS THE FOUNDER AND FIRST KING OF THE HOUSE OF PLANTAGENET, THE NAME OF WHICH DERIVED FROM THE HOUSE OF ANJOU. IT REFERS TO 'THE SPRIG OF BROOM' (*PLANTA GENISTA*) WHICH WAS HABITUALLY WORN BY GEOFFREY V, COUNT OF ANJOU AND MAINE, HENRY II'S FATHER. THE NAME OF THE HOUSE OF PLANTAGENET WAS NOT USED UNTIL THE FIFTEENTH CENTURY, HOWEVER, WHEN IT WAS ADOPTED BY RICHARD, DUKE OF YORK. (HENRY'S OWN NICKNAME OF CURTMANTLE CAME FROM THE SHORT CLOAK THAT HE WORE.)

Henry became King in 1154, even though his mother, Matilda, did not die until 1167. Through his father, he was also the heir to the region of Anjou in France, and through his marriage to Eleanor of Aquitaine (former wife of Louis VII of France) he acquired the Duchy of Aquitaine. This French inheritance meant that later English monarchs were often engaged in battles to retain their French lands, until Mary I finally lost Calais in 1558. Henry II himself devoted most of his energies towards his territories in France.

Henry II, as imagined in an engraving by an unknown artist.

Henry II strongly believed in law and order, but he faced opposition in his attempts to subject the clergy to secular law, especially from Thomas à Becket, the Archbishop of Canterbury. The crisis eventually resulted in the murder of Becket at Canterbury. Henry II's later years were much vexed by the rebellious disobedience of his sons, yet ironically his succession proved to be a straightforward matter.

Henry II's first son had died young, and his second son and namesake, known as Henry the Young King, predeceased him. He was therefore succeeded in 1189 by his third son, Richard Coeur de Lion or Lionheart, so named because of the heroic reputation he gained in the Third Crusade to recapture the Holy Land from the Muslims.

Richard I spent most of his reign abroad and he died of wounds suffered while besieging the castle of Châlus in Limousin. His wife, Berengaria of Navarre, bore him no children and was the only queen of England never to visit the country.

Richard I's youngest brother, John Lackland (so called since he lacked territory in early life), succeeded him in 1199. Feckless and unprincipled, John had been involved in conspiracies against his father and his brother. However, in the latter part of Richard I's reign, they forged friendly relations and he succeeded at his brother's request. Squabbles with the Pope led to John's excommunication (revoked in 1213), and his autocratic rule resulted in his being forced to sign the Magna Carta at Runnymede in 1215 by his nobles. This charter effectively recognized the rights and privileges of the barons, Church and freemen. John was also responsible for the murder of Arthur, son of his brother Geoffrey and the rightful heir to the throne.

John was succeeded in 1216 by his eldest son, Henry III, who was only nine years old. Henry III was regarded as a feeble figure, too easily influenced by his mother, and – like his father – at odds with the barons. In 1258 his brother-in-law Simon de Montfort, Earl of Leicester, forced him to accept the Provisions of Oxford, a system of baronial committees that supervised the government of the realm. Henry was responsible for the redesign of Westminster Abbey in 1245 by French architects, and he lived well into old age, during which time his eldest son Edward, having already proved himself to be a brave and able warrior, was groomed to take the throne.

Edward I reigned from 1272 until 1307. He was an outstanding warrior king and a great constitutional jurist, and during his reign he helped to shape many of the political

A fictitious 'portrait' of Richard I by or after the 18th-century engraver George Vertue.

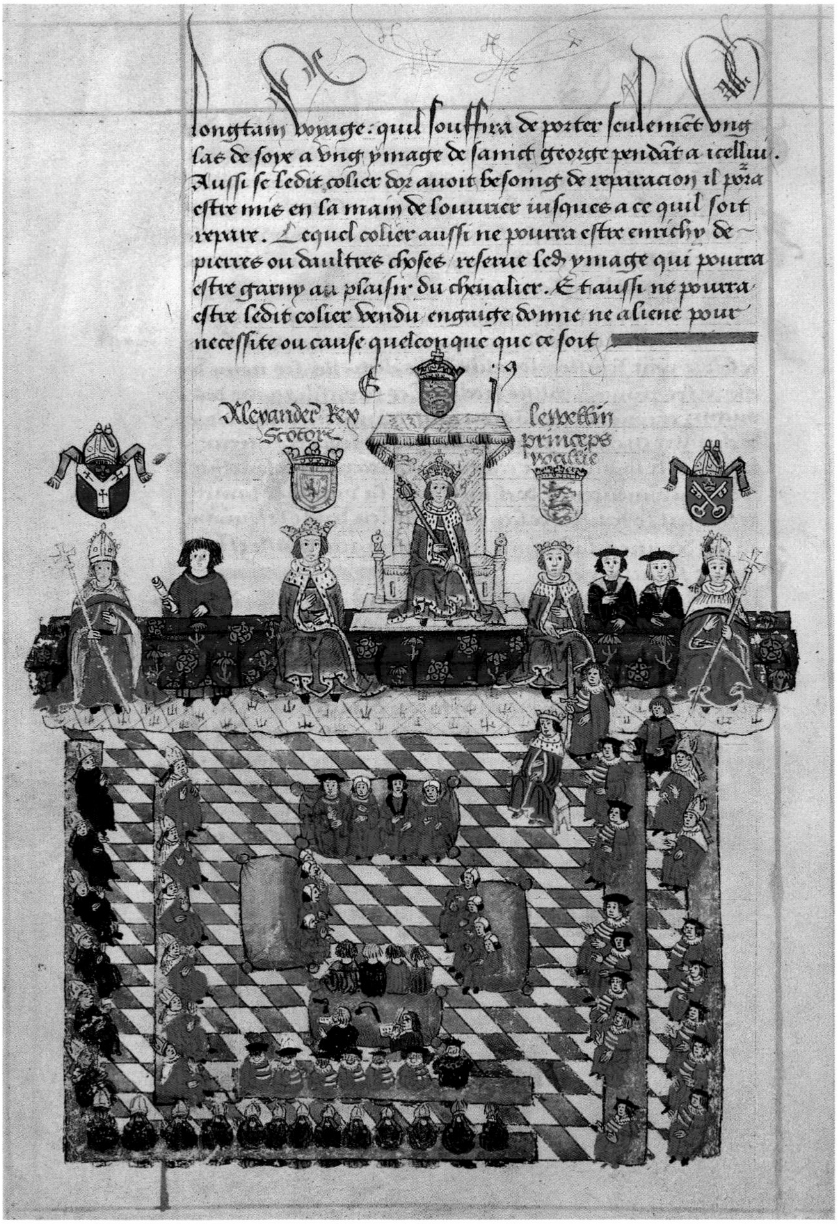

Edward I in Parliament, from the 16th-century *Wriothesley Garter Book*. The King is flanked by Alexander III of Scotland and Llywelyn the Last, Prince of Wales, who probably did not attend the same Parliament. Also shown are justices, law officers, clerks, temporal lords, bishops and abbots.

institutions of England as we know them today. He continued to assert his rule over Scotland and managed to conquer the Welsh, presenting his son Edward as the first English Prince of Wales in 1301. Edward I died near Carlisle in 1307, just as he was about to launch another attack on the Scots.

Edward's son and successor, Edward II, was known for indolence and levity; and his unpopularity grew as his favourite companion, Piers Gaveston, was given increasing importance. Edward II inherited none of his father's battle skills and was famously defeated by Robert the Bruce and the Scots at Bannockburn in 1314. He was married to Isabella of France, who for much of their marriage was estranged from him. In 1326, accompanied by her lover, Roger de Mortimer, Isabella came over from France with the plan of putting her son, also Edward, on the throne. Edward II was caught in Wales in 1327, deposed, and imprisoned in Berkeley Castle. His captors hoped he would die of disease, but his constitution proved robust. Later that year, he was ruthlessly murdered with a red-hot poker, his dying shrieks resounding through the castle.

House of Plantagenet

HENRY II (CURTMANTLE)
(1133–89)
KING OF ENGLAND
r.25 October 1154 – 6 July 1189

= 1152

Eleanor, Duchess of Aquitaine
(1122–1204)
QUEEN ELEANOR
daughter of William, Duke of Aquitain
(former wife of Louis VII, King of Franc
m. annulled 1152)

William
(1153–6)

Henry, Duke of Normandy
(The Young King)
(1155–83)
= 1160
Margaret
(1158–97/8)
daughter of Louis VII, King of France
(who m. 2ndly, 1185, Bela III,
King of Hungary)

A son
(b. & d.1177)

RICHARD I (LIONHEART)
(1157–99)
KING OF ENGLAND
r.6 July 1189 – 6 April 1199
= 1191
Berengaria
(c.1163–c.1230)
daughter of Sancho VI (The Wise),
King of Navarre

Geoffrey, Duke of Brittany
(1158–86)
(killed in a tournament in Paris)
= 1181
Constance, Duchess of Brittany
(1161–1201)
daughter of Conan IV (The Little), Duke of Brittany
(who m. 2ndly, 1186/8, diss. 1199, Ranulf, 4th Earl
of Chester, & 3rdly, 1199, Guy of Thouars)

Arthur,
Duke of Brittany
(1187–1203)
(born posthumously,
murdered at Rouen)

Eleanor
(The Damsel of Brittany)
(1184–1241)
(kept in captivity by her
uncle, King John, & cousin,
King Henry III)

Matilda
(b. & d.1185/6)

Angevins
Members of the Plantagenet line descended from Geoffrey of Anjou. The Kings of England from Henry II to Richard II (between 1154 and 1216 in particular) are often referred to as Angevins.

EDWARD I
(LONGSHANKS)
(1239–1307)
KING OF ENGLAND
r.16 November 1272 – 7 July 1307
= 1254 (1) **Eleanor**
(c.1244–90)
QUEEN ELEANOR
daughter of Fernando III,
King of Castile & Leon

= 1299 (2) **Marguerite**
(1279–1317)
QUEEN MARGUERITE
daughter of Philippe III,
King of France

Edmund Crouchback, Earl of
Leicester and of Lancaster
(1245–96)
= 1269 (1) **Aveline**
(1259–74)
daughter of William, Earl of Aumule
= 1276 (2) **Blanche**
(c.1245/50–1302)
daughter of Robert I, Count of Artois
(widow of Henri I, King of Navarre)

Richard
(b.c.1247
d. before
1256)

John
(b.c.1250
d. before
1256)

William
(b. & d.
c.1256)

Henry

Margaret
(1240–75)
= 1251
Alexander III
(1241–86)
King of Scots
(see KINGS AND QUEENS
OF SCOTLAND)

John
(1266–71)

Henry
(1267–74)

Alfonso,
Earl of
Chester
(1273–84)

EDWARD II
(1284–1327)
KING OF ENGLAND
(1st English Prince of Wales)
r.8 July 1307 – 20 January 1327
(d.21 September 1327)
= 1308
Isabella
(1295–1358)
QUEEN ISABELLA
daughter of Philippe IV, King of France

Eleanor
(1264–97)
= 1293
Henri III,
Count of Bar
(d.1302)

Joan
(b. &
d.1265)

Julian
or Katherine (?)
(b. & d.1271)

Joan of Acre
(1272–1307)
= 1290
(1) **Gilbert,**
3rd Earl of
Gloucester
(1243–95)
= 1297
(2) **Ralph,**
1st Baron
Monthermer
(d.1325/6)

Margaret
(1275–1318)
= 1290
Jean II,
Duke of
Brabant
(d.1312)

Berengaria
(1276–9)

Mary
(1278–1332)

Alice
(1279–91)

Elizabeth
(1282–1316)
= 1297 (1) **Jan I,**
Count of Holland
(d.1299)
= 1302
(2) **Humphrey de**
Bohun, 4th Earl
of Hereford &
Essex
(c.1276–1321)

Beatrice
(b.c.1286)

Bla
(b.1

EDWARD III
(1312–77)
(see HOUSES
OF LANCASTER
AND YORK)

John, Earl
of Cornwall
(1316–36)

Eleanor
(1318–55)
= 1332
Rainald II,
Duke of
Gueldres
(d.1343)

Joan
(Joan Makepeace)
(1321–62)
= 1328
David II
(1324–71)
King of Scots
(see KINGS AND
QUEENS OF
SCOTLAND)

Edward
(c.1319–c.1332)
= c.1327
Beatrice
(d.1383)
daughter of
Roger Mortimer,
1st Earl of March
(who m. 2ndly,
c.1334, Thomas, 1st
Baron Braose)

Margaret,
Duchess of Norfolk
(c.1320–1400)
= 1327
(1) **John, 4th**
Baron Segrave
(1314–53)
= 1354
(2) **Walter, 1st Baron**
Manny, KG
(c.1310–72)

Alice
(c.1324–51)
= 1339
Edward, 1st
Baron Montagu
(c.1304–61)

Edmund, 2nd
Earl of Kent
(c.1326–33)

John, 3rd
Earl of Kent
(1330–52)
= c.1352
Elizabeth
(d.1411)
daughter of
Wilhelm V,
Duke of Jülich
(who m. 2ndly,
1360, Sir Eustace
Dabridgecourt)

Joan, Countess of Kent
(The Fair Maid of Kent)
(1328–85)
= 1340 (1) **Sir Thomas de**
Holland, 1st Earl of Kent,
(d. 1360)
= 1348 (2) **William,**
2nd Earl of Salisbury, K
(1328–97)
(m. annulled 1349)
= 1361 (3) **Edward, Prince**
of Wales, KG
(The Black Prince)
(1330–76)
(see HOUSES OF
LANCASTER AND YORK)

Joan
(c.1380–1434)
= 1393
Edmund, 1st Duke of York, KG
(1341–1402)
(see HOUSES OF
LANCASTER AND YORK)
= 3 more husbands

Margaret
(1385–1439)
=
John Beaufort,
Marquess of Dorset &
Somerset, KG
(see HOUSES OF
LANCASTER AND YORK)

Arms of KING HENRY III

Arms of KING EDWARD I

Arms of KING EDWARD II

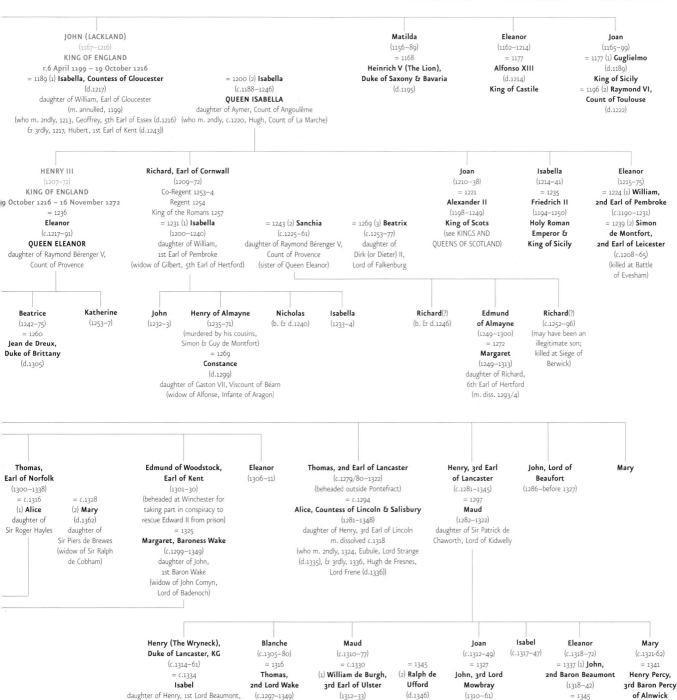

JOHN (LACKLAND)
(1167–1216)
KING OF ENGLAND
r.6 April 1199 – 19 October 1216
= 1189 (1) **Isabella, Countess of Gloucester**
(d.1217)
daughter of William, Earl of Gloucester
(m. annulled, 1199)
(who m. 2ndly, 1213, Geoffrey, 5th Earl of Essex (d.1216)
& 3rdly, 1217, Hubert, 1st Earl of Kent (d.1243))

= 1200 (2) **Isabella**
(c.1188–1246)
QUEEN ISABELLA
daughter of Aymer, Count of Angoulême
(who m. 2ndly, c.1220, Hugh, Count of La Marche)

Matilda
(1156–89)
= 1168
Heinrich V (The Lion), Duke of Saxony & Bavaria
(d.1195)

Eleanor
(1162–1214)
= 1177
Alfonso XIII
(d.1214)
King of Castile

Joan
(1165–99)
= 1177 (1) **Guglielmo**
(d.1189)
King of Sicily
= 1196 (2) **Raymond VI, Count of Toulouse**
(d.1222)

HENRY III
(1207–72)
KING OF ENGLAND
9 October 1216 – 16 November 1272
= 1236
Eleanor
(c.1217–91)
QUEEN ELEANOR
daughter of Raymond Bérenger V, Count of Provence

Richard, Earl of Cornwall
(1209–72)
Co-Regent 1253–4
Regent 1254
King of the Romans 1257
= 1231 (1) **Isabella**
(1200–1240)
daughter of William, 1st Earl of Pembroke
(widow of Gilbert, 5th Earl of Hertford)
= 1243 (2) **Sanchia**
(c.1225–61)
daughter of Raymond Bérenger V, Count of Provence
(sister of Queen Eleanor)
= 1269 (3) **Beatrix**
(c.1253–77)
daughter of Dirk (or Dieter) II, Lord of Falkenburg

Joan
(1210–38)
= 1221
Alexander II
(1198–1249)
King of Scots
(see KINGS AND QUEENS OF SCOTLAND)

Isabella
(1214–41)
= 1235
Friedrich II
(1194–1250)
Holy Roman Emperor & King of Sicily

Eleanor
(1215–75)
= 1224 (1) **William, 2nd Earl of Pembroke**
(c.1190–1231)
= 1239 (2) **Simon de Montfort, 2nd Earl of Leicester**
(c.1208–65)
(killed at Battle of Evesham)

Beatrice
(1242–75)
= 1260
Jean de Dreux, Duke of Brittany
(d.1305)

Katherine
(1253–7)

John
(1232–3)

Henry of Almayne
(1235–71)
(murdered by his cousins, Simon & Guy de Montfort)
= 1269
Constance
(d.1299)
daughter of Gaston VII, Viscount of Béarn
(widow of Alfonse, Infante of Aragon)

Nicholas
(b. & d.1240)

Isabella
(1233–4)

Richard(?)
(b. & d.1246)

Edmund of Almayne
(1249–1300)
= 1272
Margaret
(1249–1313)
daughter of Richard, 6th Earl of Hertford
(m. diss. 1293/4)

Richard(?)
(c.1252–96)
(may have been an illegitimate son; killed at Siege of Berwick)

Thomas, Earl of Norfolk
(1300–1338)
= c.1316
(1) **Alice**
daughter of Sir Roger Hayles
= c.1328
(2) **Mary**
(d.1362)
daughter of Sir Piers de Brewes
(widow of Sir Ralph de Cobham)

Edmund of Woodstock, Earl of Kent
(1301–30)
(beheaded at Winchester for taking part in conspiracy to rescue Edward II from prison)
= 1325
Margaret, Baroness Wake
(c.1299–1349)
daughter of John, 1st Baron Wake
(widow of John Comyn, Lord of Badenoch)

Eleanor
(1306–11)

Thomas, 2nd Earl of Lancaster
(c.1279/80–1322)
(beheaded outside Pontefract)
= c.1294
Alice, Countess of Lincoln & Salisbury
(1281–1348)
daughter of Henry, 3rd Earl of Lincoln
m. dissolved c.1318
(who m. 2ndly, 1324, Eubule, Lord Strange (d.1335), & 3rdly, 1336, Hugh de Fresnes, Lord Frene (d.1336))

Henry, 3rd Earl of Lancaster
(c.1281–1345)
= 1297
Maud
(1282–1322)
daughter of Sir Patrick de Chaworth, Lord of Kidwelly

John, Lord of Beaufort
(1286–before 1327)

Mary

Henry (The Wryneck), Duke of Lancaster, KG
(c.1314–61)
= c.1334
Isabel
daughter of Henry, 1st Lord Beaumont, & Earl of Buchan

Blanche
(c.1305–80)
= 1316
Thomas, 2nd Lord Wake
(c.1297–1349)

Maud
(c.1310–77)
= c.1330
(1) **William de Burgh, 3rd Earl of Ulster**
(1312–33)
(murdered at Le Ford – now Belfast)
= 1345
(2) **Ralph de Ufford**
(d.1346)

Joan
(c.1312–49)
= 1327
John, 3rd Lord Mowbray
(1310–61)

Isabel
(c.1317–47)

Eleanor
(c.1318–72)
= 1337 (1) **John, 2nd Baron Beaumont**
(1318–42)
= 1345
(2) **Richard Fitzalan, 10th Earl of Arundel, KG**
(c.1313–76)

Mary
(c.1321-62)
= 1341
Henry Percy, 3rd Baron Percy of Alnwick
(c.1320–68)

mas de Holland, 2nd Earl of Kent, KG
(c.1350–97)
= 1364
Alice
(d.1415/16)
hter of Richard, Earl of Arundel

John de Holland 1st Duke of Exeter, KG
(c.1350–1400, beheaded)
= c.1386
Elizabeth
(c.1363–1425)
daughter of John of Gaunt, Duke of Lancaster

Maud (Matilda)
(1335–62)
= 1344 (1) **Ralph Stafford**
(d.1349)
= 1352 (2) **Wilhelm I, Duke of Bavaria**
(d.1389)

Blanche
(1345–69)
= 1359
John of Gaunt, Duke of Lancaster, KG
(1340–99)
(see HOUSES OF LANCASTER AND YORK)

Elizabeth de Burgh
(1332–63)
= 1342
Lionel, Duke of Clarence, KG
(1338–68)
(see HOUSES OF LANCASTER AND YORK)

Houses of Lancaster and York

THE LINE OF DESCENT FROM EDWARD III (1327–77) TO HENRY VII RUNS THROUGH 150 YEARS OR SO OF SOME OF THE MOST DRAMATIC EVENTS AND CONFLICTS IN THE HISTORY OF ENGLAND.

Edward III is notable for having founded the Order of the Garter (the senior order of British chivalry) in 1348. Placed on the throne by his mother, Queen Isabella, and her lover Roger de Mortimer, the King was married to Philippa of Hainault at their instigation, although it proved to be a happy marriage. Edward III laid claim to the kingdom of France through his mother and, aided by his son Edward, won victories at the Battle of Crécy (1346) and the conquest of Calais (1347). These conflicts were the start of the Hundred Years War between England and France.

Edward III had seven sons, of whom five played a significant part in history: Edward, the Black Prince; Lionel, Duke of Clarence (the Yorkist party based their claim to the throne on descent from Philippa, his daughter by his first marriage); John of Gaunt, Duke of Lancaster; Edmund, Duke of York; and Thomas, Duke of Gloucester. The rivalry that sprang up between their descendants led to the Wars of the Roses.

The Black Prince died in 1376, so on the death of Edward III in the following year the throne passed to the Black Prince's surviving son, Richard II. In 1381, when only fourteen, Richard bravely quelled the Peasants' Revolt led by Wat Tyler. Richard's uncles were constantly jostling for power and for a long time Thomas, Duke of Gloucester, held considerable sway at court. Later, with the help of another uncle, John of Gaunt, Richard overthrew Gloucester and his supporters. Richard II reigned until he was coerced into giving up the throne in September 1399 by his first cousin, Henry, Duke of Lancaster. Henry was the son of John of Gaunt (who had died in February 1399). Richard died in prison at Pontefract Castle in February 1400.

Edward III with the Black Prince after the Battle of Crécy, Benjamin West, 1788. The Black Prince was the hero of the battles of Crécy (1346) and Poitiers (1356).

Parliament consented to Henry, Duke of Lancaster, becoming King – Richard II had been childless – and, as Henry IV, he was the first King of the House of Lancaster. His son, Henry V, who came to power in 1413, is best remembered for his great victory against the French at Agincourt in 1415, and for realizing the importance to Britain of sea power. He reigned until 1422, and was duly succeeded by his son, Henry VI, during whose reign the French expelled the English from most of northern France. Henry VI was considered weak, and was plagued by intermittent periods of insanity. During these periods Richard, 3rd Duke of York, served as Protector (1454–5 and 1455–6). Open rivalries between the Duke of York and Edmund, 1st Duke of Somerset, erupted into the bloody conflict known as the Wars of the Roses (1455–85), named after the heraldic badges of the Houses of York and Lancaster.

During the course of these wars, Richard, Duke of York, captured Henry VI at Northampton in 1460 and forced Henry to acknowledge him as Protector and Defender of the Realm. In the same year Richard was killed in battle, and in the following year, 1461, his son deposed Henry VI and succeeded as Edward IV.

Henry VI took refuge in Scotland, was captured and was imprisoned in the Tower of London in 1464, but was re-placed on the throne briefly in 1470 by Richard Neville the Kingmaker, 1st Earl of Warwick. But Edward IV crushed the Lancastrians at the battles of Barnet and Tewkesbury in 1471, killed Edward, Prince of Wales, and had Henry secretly murdered. In this way, Edward IV recovered the throne (retaining it until his death in 1483) and became the first Sovereign of the House of York. He was also the first King to address Parliament in person. He allowed many great nobles to build large power bases in the provinces in return for their support.

In 1483 the crown passed to Edward V, the oldest son of Edward IV, then a boy of twelve. His guardian was his uncle, Richard, Duke of Gloucester (who, it was said, had already been responsible for drowning his own elder brother, George, Duke of Clarence, in a butt of Malmsey wine for siding with the Earl of Warwick). Later that year Edward V was imprisoned in the Tower with his brother Richard, Duke of York, and they were never seen in public again. Although Richard III has been blamed for their murders, there has also been a lasting theory that they survived his reign and that it was the future Henry VII who had them killed.

The Duke of Gloucester succeeded to the throne as Richard III, and reigned for two years between 1483 and 1485. The death of Richard III's ten-year-old son in 1484 prompted him to nominate his nephew, John, Earl of Lincoln, as heir. However, the Lancastrians put forward their own champion, Henry Tudor, Earl of Richmond, whose mother, Margaret Beaufort, descended from the only surviving branch of the House of Lancaster. It was a weak claim as Henry's mother was a descendant of John of Gaunt's third marriage, the children of which had been born out of wedlock. They were legitimized by royal charter in 1397 but barred from succession to the throne.

Henry defeated Richard III's armies at the Battle of Bosworth (where Richard was killed), and he mounted the throne as Henry VII, his title being confirmed by an Act of Parliament. Wisely, he married Elizabeth, eldest daughter of Edward IV and heiress of the House of York, thus uniting the rival claims of Edward III's descendants to form the new Tudor dynasty.

LEFT: *Richard II*, unknown artist, 1390s
ABOVE: *Henry IV*, British School, 16th century

Henry VI, British School, 16th century

ABOVE: *The Marriage of Henry V and Catherine of France, 1420*, William Kent, 1729

LEFT: *Richard III*, British School, 16th century

Edward IV, Anglo-Flemish School, 16th century

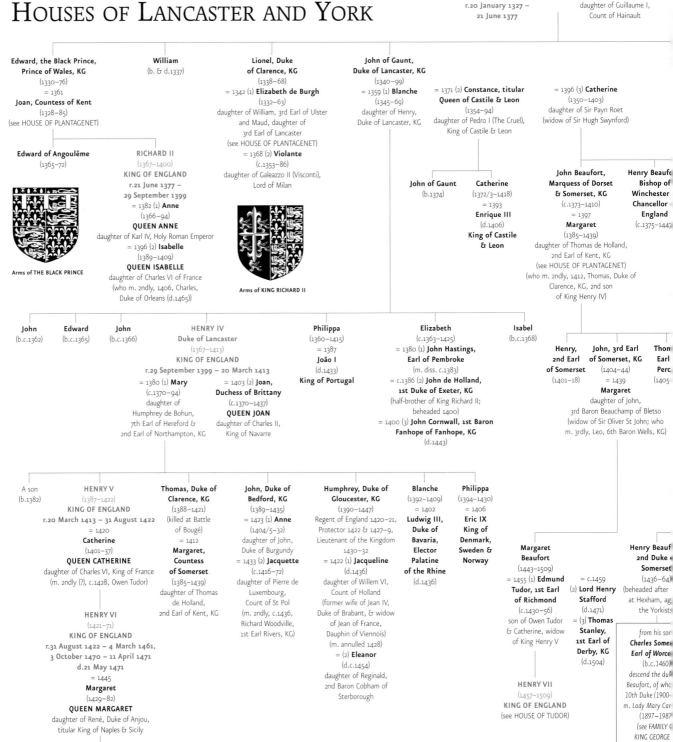

Houses of Lancaster and York

EDWARD III
(1312–77)
KING OF ENGLAND
r.20 January 1327 – 21 June 1377
= 1328
Philippa
(c.1312–69)
QUEEN PHILIPPA
daughter of Guillaume I, Count of Hainault

Edward, the Black Prince, Prince of Wales, KG
(1330–76)
= 1361
Joan, Countess of Kent
(1328–85)
(see HOUSE OF PLANTAGENET)

William
(b. & d.1337)

Lionel, Duke of Clarence, KG
(1338–68)
= 1342 (1) **Elizabeth de Burgh**
(1332–63)
daughter of William, 3rd Earl of Ulster and Maud, daughter of 3rd Earl of Lancaster
(see HOUSE OF PLANTAGENET)
= 1368 (2) **Violante**
(c.1353–86)
daughter of Galeazzo II (Visconti), Lord of Milan

John of Gaunt, Duke of Lancaster, KG
(1340–99)
= 1359 (1) **Blanche**
(1345–69)
daughter of Henry, Duke of Lancaster, KG
= 1371 (2) **Constance, titular Queen of Castile & Leon**
(1354–94)
daughter of Pedro I (The Cruel), King of Castile & Leon
= 1396 (3) **Catherine**
(1350–1403)
daughter of Sir Payn Roet
(widow of Sir Hugh Swynford)

Edward of Angoulême
(1365–72)

RICHARD II
(1367–1400)
KING OF ENGLAND
r.21 June 1377 – 29 September 1399
= 1382 (1) **Anne**
(1366–94)
QUEEN ANNE
daughter of Karl IV, Holy Roman Emperor
= 1396 (2) **Isabelle**
(1389–1409)
QUEEN ISABELLE
daughter of Charles VI of France
(who m. 2ndly, 1406, Charles, Duke of Orleans (d.1465))

Arms of THE BLACK PRINCE

Arms of KING RICHARD II

John of Gaunt
(b.1374)

Catherine
(1372/3–1418)
= 1393
Enrique III
(d.1406)
King of Castile & Leon

John Beaufort, Marquess of Dorset & Somerset, KG
(c.1373–1410)
= 1397
Margaret
(1385–1439)
daughter of Thomas de Holland, 2nd Earl of Kent, KG
(see HOUSE OF PLANTAGENET)
(who m. 2ndly, 1412, Thomas, Duke of Clarence, KG, 2nd son of King Henry IV)

Henry Beauf
Bishop of
Winchester
Chancellor
England
(c.1375–1447

John
(b.c.1362)

Edward
(b.c.1365)

John
(b.c.1366)

HENRY IV
Duke of Lancaster
(1367–1413)
KING OF ENGLAND
r.29 September 1399 – 20 March 1413
= 1380 (1) **Mary**
(c.1370–94)
daughter of Humphrey de Bohun, 7th Earl of Hereford & 2nd Earl of Northampton, KG
= 1403 (2) **Joan, Duchess of Brittany**
(c.1370–1437)
QUEEN JOAN
daughter of Charles II, King of Navarre

Philippa
(1360–1415)
= 1387
João I
(d.1433)
King of Portugal

Elizabeth
(c.1363–1425)
= 1380 (1) **John Hastings, Earl of Pembroke**
(m. diss. c.1383)
= c.1386 (2) **John de Holland, 1st Duke of Exeter, KG**
(half-brother of King Richard II; beheaded 1400)
= 1400 (3) **John Cornwall, 1st Baron Fanhope of Fanhope, KG**
(d.1443)

Isabel
(b.c.1368)

Henry, 2nd Earl of Somerset
(1401–18)

John, 3rd Earl of Somerset, KG
(1404–44)
= 1439
Margaret
daughter of John, 3rd Baron Beauchamp of Bletso
(widow of Sir Oliver St John; who m. 3rdly, Leo, 6th Baron Wells, KG)

Thom
Earl
Perc
(1405

A son
(b.1382)

HENRY V
(1387–1422)
KING OF ENGLAND
r.20 March 1413 – 31 August 1422
= 1420
Catherine
(1401–37)
QUEEN CATHERINE
daughter of Charles VI, King of France
(m. 2ndly (?), c.1428, Owen Tudor)

Thomas, Duke of Clarence, KG
(1388–1421)
(killed at Battle of Bougé)
= 1412
Margaret, Countess of Somerset
(1385–1439)
daughter of Thomas de Holland, 2nd Earl of Kent, KG

John, Duke of Bedford, KG
(1389–1435)
= 1423 (1) **Anne**
(1404/5–32)
daughter of John, Duke of Burgundy
= 1433 (2) **Jacquette**
(c.1416–72)
daughter of Pierre de Luxembourg, Count of St Pol
(m. 2ndly, c.1436, Richard Woodville, 1st Earl Rivers, KG)

Humphrey, Duke of Gloucester, KG
(1390–1447)
Regent of England 1420–21, Protector 1422 & 1427–9, Lieutenant of the Kingdom 1430–32
= 1422 (1) **Jacqueline**
(d.1436)
daughter of Willem VI, Count of Holland
(former wife of Jean IV, Duke of Brabant, & widow of Jean of France, Dauphin of Viennois)
(m. annulled 1428)
= (2) **Eleanor**
(d.c.1454)
daughter of Reginald, 2nd Baron Cobham of Sterborough

Blanche
(1392–1409)
= 1402
Ludwig III, Duke of Bavaria, Elector Palatine of the Rhine
(d.1436)

Philippa
(1394–1430)
= 1406
Eric IX King of Denmark, Sweden & Norway

Margaret Beaufort
(1443–1509)
= 1455 (1) **Edmund Tudor, 1st Earl of Richmond**
(c.1430–56)
son of Owen Tudor & Catherine, widow of King Henry V
= c.1459 (2) **Lord Henry Stafford**
(d.1471)
= (3) **Thomas Stanley, 1st Earl of Derby, KG**
(d.1504)

Henry Beauf
2nd Duke
Somerset
(1436–64
(beheaded after at Hexham, ag the Yorkist

from his son
Charles Some
Earl of Worce
(b.c.1460)
descend the du
Beaufort, of who
10th Duke (1900–
m. Lady Mary Car
(1897–1987
(see FAMILY
KING GEORGE

HENRY VI
(1421–71)
KING OF ENGLAND
r.31 August 1422 – 4 March 1461, 3 October 1470 – 11 April 1471
d.21 May 1471
= 1445
Margaret
(1429–82)
QUEEN MARGARET
daughter of René, Duke of Anjou, titular King of Naples & Sicily

HENRY VII
(1457–1509)
KING OF ENGLAND
(see HOUSE OF TUDOR)

Edward, Prince of Wales
(1453–71)
= 1470
Anne
(1456–85)
daughter of Richard, 1st Earl of Warwick & 2nd Earl of Salisbury, KG
(m. 2ndly, 1472, Richard, Duke of Gloucester, later King Richard III)

EDWARD V
(1470–c.1483)
KING OF ENGLAND
r.9 April – 25 June 1483
(presumed murdered in the Tower of London)

Richard, Duke of York, KG
(1473–c.1483)
(presumed murdered in the Tower of London)
= 1478
Anne
(1472–81)
daughter of John Mowbray, 4th Duke of Norfolk, KG

George, Duke of Bedford
(1477–9)

Elizabeth
(1466–1503)
= 1486
HENRY VII
(1457–1509)
KING OF ENGLAND
(see HOUSE OF TUDOR)

Mary
(1467–82)

Cicely
(1469–150
= 1487
(1) **John, 1**
Viscount
Welles, K
(d.1499)
= 1504
(2) **Thomas K**

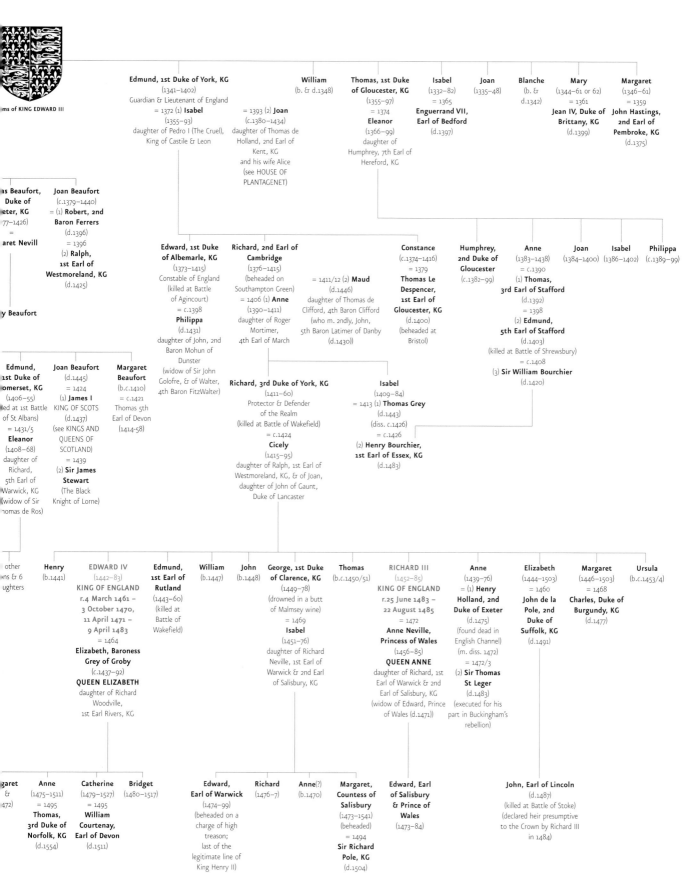

ms of KING EDWARD III

Edmund, 1st Duke of York, KG
(1341–1402)
Guardian & Lieutenant of England
= 1372 (1) Isabel
(1355–93)
daughter of Pedro I (The Cruel), King of Castile & Leon
= 1393 (2) Joan
(c.1380–1434)
daughter of Thomas de Holland, 2nd Earl of Kent, KG
and his wife Alice
(see HOUSE OF PLANTAGENET)

William
(b. & d.1348)

Thomas, 1st Duke of Gloucester, KG
(1355–97)
= 1374
Eleanor
(1366–99)
daughter of Humphrey, 7th Earl of Hereford, KG

Isabel
(1332–82)
= 1365
Enguerrand VII, Earl of Bedford
(d.1397)

Joan
(1335–48)

Blanche
(b. & d.1342)

Mary
(1344–61 or 62)
= 1361
Jean IV, Duke of Brittany, KG
(d.1399)

Margaret
(1346–61)
= 1359
John Hastings, 2nd Earl of Pembroke, KG
(d.1375)

---

as Beaufort, Duke of eter, KG
77–1426)
=
aret Nevill

y Beaufort

Joan Beaufort
(c.1379–1440)
= (1) Robert, 2nd Baron Ferrers
(d.1396)
= 1396
(2) Ralph, 1st Earl of Westmoreland, KG
(d.1425)

Edward, 1st Duke of Albemarle, KG
(1373–1415)
Constable of England
(killed at Battle of Agincourt)
= c.1398
Philippa
(d.1431)
daughter of John, 2nd Baron Mohun of Dunster
(widow of Sir John Golofre, & of Walter, 4th Baron FitzWalter)

Richard, 2nd Earl of Cambridge
(1376–1415)
(beheaded on Southampton Green)
= 1406 (1) Anne
(1390–1411)
daughter of Roger Mortimer, 4th Earl of March
= 1411/12 (2) Maud
(d.1446)
daughter of Thomas de Clifford, 4th Baron Clifford
(who m. 2ndly, John, 5th Baron Latimer of Danby
(d.1430))

Constance
(c.1374–1416)
= 1379
Thomas Le Despencer, 1st Earl of Gloucester, KG
(d.1400)
(beheaded at Bristol)

Humphrey, 2nd Duke of Gloucester
(c.1382–99)

Anne
(1383–1438)
= c.1390
(1) Thomas, 3rd Earl of Stafford
(d.1392)
= 1398
(2) Edmund, 5th Earl of Stafford
(d.1403)
(killed at Battle of Shrewsbury)
= c.1408
(3) Sir William Bourchier
(d.1420)

Joan
(1384–1400)

Isabel
(1386–1402)

Philippa
(c.1389–99)

Edmund, 1st Duke of omerset, KG
(1406–55)
led at 1st Battle of St Albans)
= 1431/5
Eleanor
(1408–68)
daughter of Richard, 5th Earl of Warwick, KG
(widow of Sir homas de Ros)

Joan Beaufort
(d.1445)
= 1424
(1) James I KING OF SCOTS
(d.1437)
(see KINGS AND QUEENS OF SCOTLAND)
= 1439
(2) Sir James Stewart
(The Black Knight of Lorne)

Margaret Beaufort
(b.c.1410)
= c.1421
Thomas 5th Earl of Devon
(1414-58)

Richard, 3rd Duke of York, KG
(1411–60)
Protector & Defender of the Realm
(killed at Battle of Wakefield)
= c.1424
Cicely
(1415–95)
daughter of Ralph, 1st Earl of Westmoreland, KG, & of Joan, daughter of John of Gaunt, Duke of Lancaster

Isabel
(1409–84)
= 1413 (1) Thomas Grey
(d.1443)
(diss. c.1426)
= c.1426
(2) Henry Bourchier, 1st Earl of Essex, KG
(d.1483)

---

other ns & 6 ughters

Henry
(b.1441)

EDWARD IV
(1442–83)
KING OF ENGLAND
r.4 March 1461 – 3 October 1470, 11 April 1471 – 9 April 1483
= 1464
Elizabeth, Baroness Grey of Groby
(c.1437–92)
QUEEN ELIZABETH
daughter of Richard Woodville, 1st Earl Rivers, KG

Edmund, 1st Earl of Rutland
(1443–60)
(killed at Battle of Wakefield)

William
(b.1447)

John
(b.1448)

George, 1st Duke of Clarence, KG
(1449–78)
(drowned in a butt of Malmsey wine)
= 1469
Isabel
(1451–76)
daughter of Richard Neville, 1st Earl of Warwick & 2nd Earl of Salisbury, KG

Thomas
(b.c.1450/51)

RICHARD III
(1452–85)
KING OF ENGLAND
r.25 June 1483 – 22 August 1485
= 1472
Anne Neville, Princess of Wales
(1456–85)
QUEEN ANNE
daughter of Richard, 1st Earl of Warwick & 2nd Earl of Salisbury, KG
(widow of Edward, Prince of Wales (d.1471))

Anne
(1439–76)
= (1) Henry Holland, 2nd Duke of Exeter
(d.1475)
(found dead in English Channel)
(m. diss. 1472)
= 1472/3
(2) Sir Thomas St Leger
(d.1483)
(executed for his part in Buckingham's rebellion)

Elizabeth
(1444–1503)
= 1460
John de la Pole, 2nd Duke of Suffolk, KG
(d.1491)

Margaret
(1446–1503)
= 1468
Charles, Duke of Burgundy, KG
(d.1477)

Ursula
(b.c.1453/4)

---

garet & 472)

Anne
(1475–1511)
= 1495
Thomas, 3rd Duke of Norfolk, KG
(d.1554)

Catherine
(1479–1527)
= 1495
William Courtenay, Earl of Devon
(d.1511)

Bridget
(1480–1517)

Edward, Earl of Warwick
(1474–99)
(beheaded on a charge of high treason; last of the legitimate line of King Henry II)

Richard
(1476–7)

Anne(?)
(b.1470)

Margaret, Countess of Salisbury
(1473–1541)
(beheaded)
= 1494
Sir Richard Pole, KG
(d.1504)

Edward, Earl of Salisbury & Prince of Wales
(1473–84)

John, Earl of Lincoln
(d.1487)
(killed at Battle of Stoke)
(declared heir presumptive to the Crown by Richard III in 1484)

House of Tudor

THE HOUSE OF TUDOR LASTED FOR NEARLY 120 YEARS, BUT COMPRISED ONLY THREE GENERATIONS (OR FOUR, INCLUDING LADY JANE GREY). HENRY VII'S WIFE, ELIZABETH OF YORK, WAS THE DAUGHTER OF EDWARD IV, THE SISTER OF EDWARD V, AND BY 1485 THE HEIR TO THE HOUSE OF YORK. THUS THE 'RED ROSE' OF LANCASTER FINALLY UNITED WITH THE 'WHITE ROSE' OF YORK, GIVING THEIR DESCENDANTS AN INALIENABLE RIGHT TO SIT ON THE THRONE OF ENGLAND. HENRY DESCENDED FROM THE KINGS OF FRANCE AND THE NATIVE PRINCES OF WALES THROUGH HIS FATHER, EDMUND TUDOR.

Henry VII, unknown artist, 16th century

Henry VII's paternal grandmother was Catherine of France, daughter of King Charles VI. His mother, Lady Margaret Beaufort, was alive when he took the throne, and in fact outlived her son by three months.

Henry VII enjoyed a successful reign and concentrated on maintaining stability in the country after years of warfare. He undertook many building projects and founded religious houses. His son and heir, Arthur, Prince of Wales, married Catherine of Aragon but died at the age of fifteen in 1502. Arthur's brother succeeded as Henry VIII in 1509.

Henry VIII's life was dominated by the need to produce a male heir. He married his brother's widow in 1509. Catherine produced six children, but only one child – a daughter – survived, subsequently becoming Mary I. Henry broke from Rome after the Pope refused to annul his marriage, and divorced Catherine in order to marry Anne Boleyn, who bore him the future Elizabeth I. Anne Boleyn was executed on a charge of adultery and Henry then married Jane Seymour, the mother of Edward VI. Jane died shortly after giving birth, and there were three subsequent Queens: Anne of Cleves, whom Henry VIII divorced; Catherine Howard, who was executed; and Catherine Parr, who survived the King.

An extravagant figure with a Renaissance education, Henry looms large over history. By the Acts of Annates, Appeals and Supremacy, he declared himself Supreme Head of the Church and, by no longer paying funds into the papal treasury, he repudiated the Pope's ecclesiastical authority in England. These radical changes to the Church continued with the Dissolution of the Monasteries in 1536 and 1539. Henry also united Wales with England by the Statutes of Wales of 1534–6.

Henry VIII was succeeded by his only son Edward VI, then aged only nine. Edward's short reign was overshadowed by the protectorate of his maternal uncle, the Duke of Somerset (to whose execution Edward assented in 1552), and then by that of John Dudley, Earl of Warwick, created Duke of Northumberland in 1551. Edward VI died at Greenwich in 1553 at the age of fifteen.

Edward VI named as his successor Lady Jane Grey, who was the granddaughter of Henry VII's third daughter, Mary. Henry VIII had left the crown to Mary's descendants, rather than those of his elder sister, Margaret, Queen of Scotland, should his own issue fail. Lady Jane Grey's accession threatened the senior lineal heirs, Mary and Elizabeth, and the royal House of Scotland, which descended from Margaret.

The Duke of Northumberland arranged Lady Jane's marriage to his son, Guilford Dudley, and set up his reluctant daughter-in-law on the throne on the grounds that Mary and Elizabeth had both been declared illegitimate. However, the country rallied behind Mary Tudor, the rightful Queen. Jane was overthrown; she was executed with her husband at the Tower of London in February 1554, her reign having lasted only nine days.

Mary I had been in line to the throne, but after her mother's death in 1536 she was forced to sign a declaration acknowledging that her parents' union had been illegal and that she was illegitimate. After Edward VI died, Mary's claim to the throne was recognized and she was crowned in 1553.

Mary, a devout Catholic, was much influenced by her cousin, Emperor Charles V, and she married his son, Philip II of Spain, thereby alienating the English people. Her determination to restore papal supremacy led to a rebellion (quelled in 1554) and a phase of religious persecutions that earned her the nickname of Bloody Mary. Deserted by Philip in 1557, she died childless a year later.

Mary I's half-sister and successor was the last of the Tudors. Like Mary, Elizabeth had been declared illegitimate when her mother fell from grace, but her reign as Elizabeth I, the Virgin Queen, is remembered as a glorious one, notable for the victory of the English fleet over the Spanish Armada in 1588 and the flowering of the English Renaissance.

Elizabeth never married, and on her death the succession was again in doubt. In the end, despite the threat which had been posed by Mary, Queen of Scots, to the English throne (Elizabeth had her cousin executed in 1587), it was to Mary's son, James VI of Scotland, that Elizabeth entrusted her kingdom.

Henry VIII, after Hans Holbein the Younger, 16th century

Edward VI, Flemish School, c.1546

FAR LEFT: *Mary I*, after Anthonis Mor, 1553/4. The original of this portrait is in the Prado, Madrid.

LEFT: *Elizabeth I*, unknown artist, 16th century

House of Tudor

HENRY VII
(1457–1509)
KING OF ENGLAND
r.22 August 1485 – 21 April 1509

= 1486

Princess Elizabeth of York
(1466–1503)
QUEEN ELIZABETH
daughter of King Edward IV
(see HOUSES OF LANCASTER AND YORK)

Arthur, Prince of Wales, KG
(1486–1502)
= 1501
Catherine of Aragon
(1485–1536)
daughter of Ferdinand V, King of Aragon, and Isabelle I, Queen of Castile & Leon

HENRY VIII
(1491–1547)
KING OF ENGLAND
r.21 April 1509 – 28 January 1547

= 1509 (1) **Catherine of Aragon**
(1485–1536)
Princess of Wales
QUEEN CATHERINE
(m. declared null 1533, diss. 1534)

= 1533 (2) **Anne Boleyn, Marchioness of Pembroke**
(c.1501/2–36)
daughter of Thomas Boleyn, 1st Earl of Wiltshire & Ormonde, KG
QUEEN ANNE
(m. declared invalid 1536; beheaded)

= 1536
(3) **Jane Seymour**
(c.1505–37)
daughter of Sir John Seymour
QUEEN JANE

= 1540
(4) **Anne of Cleves**
(1515–57)
daughter of Johann III, Duke of Cleves
QUEEN ANNE
(m. annulled 1540)

= 1540
(5) **Catherine Howa**
(1521/2–42)
daughter of Lord Edm
Howard (son of Thomas H
2nd Duke of Norfolk,
QUEEN CATHERIN
(beheaded)

Children of Henry VIII and Catherine of Aragon:

Henry, Duke of Cornwall
(b. & d.1511)

A son (Henry?), Duke of Cornwall
(b. & d.1513)

A son
(1514)
(stillborn?)

A daughter
(1510)
(stillborn)

MARY I
(1516–58)
QUEEN OF ENGLAND
r.19 July 1553 – 17 November 1558
= 1554
PHILIP II
King of Spain
(1527–98)

A daughter
(1518)
(stillborn)

Children of Henry VIII and Anne Boleyn:

A son
(1536)
(stillborn)

ELIZABETH I
(1533–1603)
QUEEN OF ENGLAND
r.17 November 1558 – 24 March 1603

Child of Henry VIII and Jane Seymour:

EDWARD VI
(1537–53)
KING OF ENGLAND
r.28 January 1547 – 6 July 1553

Catherine of Aragon, unknown artist

Anne Boleyn, unknown artist

Jane Seymour, Hans Holbein

Anne of Cleves, Hans Holbein

Catherine Howard, Hans Holbein

Catherine Parr, William Scrots

Arms of HENRY VI, VII and VIII

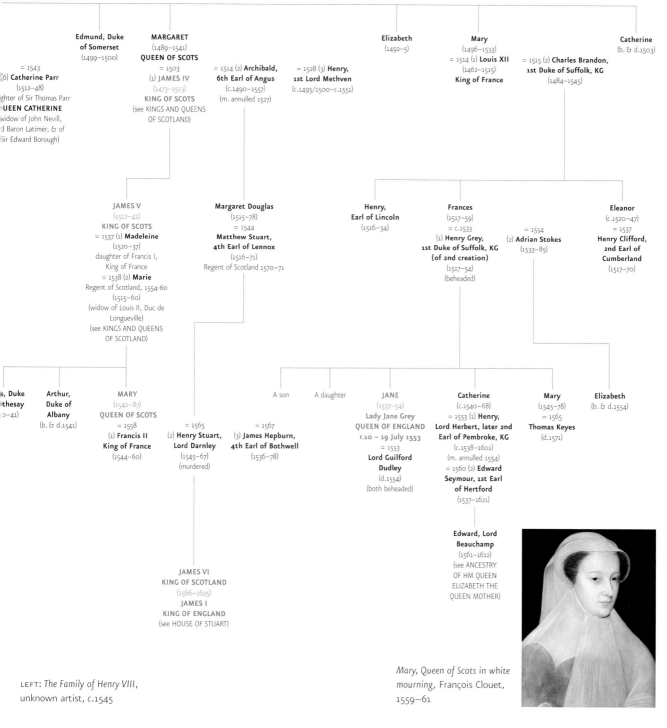

= 1543
(6) Catherine Parr
(1512–48)
…ghter of Sir Thomas Parr
…UEEN CATHERINE
…widow of John Nevill,
…d Baron Latimer, & of
…Sir Edward Borough)

Edmund, Duke of Somerset
(1499–1500)

MARGARET
(1489–1541)
QUEEN OF SCOTS
= 1503
(1) JAMES IV
(1473–1513)
KING OF SCOTS
(see KINGS AND QUEENS OF SCOTLAND)

= 1514 (2) Archibald, 6th Earl of Angus
(c.1490–1557)
(m. annulled 1527)

= 1528 (3) Henry, 1st Lord Methven
(c.1495/1500–c.1551)

Elizabeth
(1492–5)

Mary
(1496–1533)
= 1514 (1) Louis XII
(1462–1515)
King of France

= 1515 (2) Charles Brandon, 1st Duke of Suffolk, KG
(1484–1545)

Catherine
(b. & d.1503)

JAMES V
(1512–42)
KING OF SCOTS
= 1537 (1) Madeleine
(1520–37)
daughter of Francis I, King of France
= 1538 (2) Marie
Regent of Scotland, 1554-60
(1515–60)
(widow of Louis II, Duc de Longueville)
(see KINGS AND QUEENS OF SCOTLAND)

Margaret Douglas
(1515–78)
= 1544
Matthew Stuart, 4th Earl of Lennox
(1516–71)
Regent of Scotland 1570–71

Henry, Earl of Lincoln
(1516–34)

Frances
(1517–59)
= c.1533
(1) Henry Grey, 1st Duke of Suffolk, KG (of 2nd creation)
(1517–54)
(beheaded)

= 1554
(2) Adrian Stokes
(1533–85)

Eleanor
(c.1520–47)
= 1537
Henry Clifford, 2nd Earl of Cumberland
(1517–70)

…, Duke …thesay
(…–41)

Arthur, Duke of Albany
(b. & d.1541)

MARY
(1542–87)
QUEEN OF SCOTS
= 1558
(1) Francis II
King of France
(1544–60)

= 1565
(2) Henry Stuart, Lord Darnley
(1545–67)
(murdered)

= 1567
(3) James Hepburn, 4th Earl of Bothwell
(1536–78)

A son

A daughter

JANE
(1537–54)
Lady Jane Grey
QUEEN OF ENGLAND
r.10 – 19 July 1553
= 1553
Lord Guilford Dudley
(d.1554)
(both beheaded)

Catherine
(c.1540–68)
= 1553 (1) Henry, Lord Herbert, later 2nd Earl of Pembroke, KG
(c.1538–1601)
(m. annulled 1554)
= 1560 (2) Edward Seymour, 1st Earl of Hertford
(1537–1621)

Mary
(1545–78)
= 1565
Thomas Keyes
(d.1571)

Elizabeth
(b. & d.1554)

Edward, Lord Beauchamp
(1561–1612)
(see ANCESTRY OF HM QUEEN ELIZABETH THE QUEEN MOTHER)

JAMES VI
KING OF SCOTLAND
(1566–1625)
JAMES I
KING OF ENGLAND
(see HOUSE OF STUART)

LEFT: *The Family of Henry VIII*, unknown artist, c.1545

Mary, Queen of Scots in white mourning, François Clouet, 1559–61

House of Stuart

JAMES VI, KING OF SCOTLAND, BECAME JAMES I OF ENGLAND IN 1603 AND THE TWO COUNTRIES THEREAFTER SHARED A MONARCH. JAMES WAS MARRIED TO ANNE OF DENMARK, WHO BORE HIM EIGHT CHILDREN, THREE OF WHOM SURVIVED INFANCY. JAMES I'S ELDEST SON, HENRY FREDERICK, PRINCE OF WALES, PREDECEASED HIM IN 1612, AND JAMES WAS THEREFORE SUCCEEDED BY HIS SECOND SON, WHO BECAME CHARLES I. JAMES I'S DAUGHTER ELIZABETH WAS THE SOURCE OF THE HANOVERIAN SUCCESSION. HER GRANDSON WAS GEORGE I.

Charles I was cultured and a great patron of the arts, but his reign was overshadowed by his conflicts with Parliament. The dissolution of Parliament in 1629 was followed by eleven years of the King's personal rule. Civil war broke out in England in 1642, leading to the King's eventual defeat at the hands of Oliver Cromwell (1599–1658) in 1646. Charles I was executed in Whitehall in 1649, and there then occurred the only break in the long monarchic succession, when England became a republic under Oliver Cromwell.

James I, Paul van Somer, *c.*1620

Parliament declared England to be a Commonwealth, and consigned the powers of government to a reformed House of Commons and a Council of State. In reality, power lay with the army and Oliver Cromwell, who became Lord Protector in 1653. Cromwell died in 1658 and was buried in Westminster Abbey. (At the Restoration in 1660 his body was disinterred, dragged to Tyburn and beheaded; his head was stuck on a pike at Westminster, where it remained for twenty years.) His son Richard Cromwell was proclaimed Protector but proved unfit to rule, and abdicated in 1659.

Meanwhile, Charles II had escaped abroad. Following his father's execution, he returned with an army and was crowned King at Scone on 1 January 1651. He then marched on to England but was defeated by Cromwell at the Battle of Worcester, and fled into exile. In May 1660 Charles made a triumphant return to London, thus ending England's only experience of a republican government.

Charles II had to work hard, particularly to mend the religious divisions that his father had created. Royal powers and privileges had been severely limited by Parliament. This was a turning point in English history as Parliament maintained a superior position to that of the King; and from the roots of the Cavaliers and Roundheads of the Civil War grew the concept of political parties as we know them today. Charles II reigned until 1685, having fathered many illegitimate children, and was the ancestor of two members of the British Royal Family: Princess Alice, Duchess of Gloucester (Queen Elizabeth II's aunt, see page 52), and Diana, Princess of Wales (who had three lines of descent from Charles II, see pages 60–61). Charles II was a charismatic and pragmatic monarch. His otherwise successful reign was blighted by the Great Plague in 1665 and the Great Fire of London a year later.

As Charles II had no legitimate children, in 1685 he was succeeded by his brother, James II, who was a Catholic. James had married as his first wife the Protestant Anne Hyde, daughter of Charles II's Lord Chancellor, Lord Clarendon. Their daughter Mary, also a Protestant, was James's heir and was married to her Dutch Protestant cousin, William, Prince of Orange.

Charles I in three positions, Sir Anthony Van Dyck, 1635–6. This famous triple portrait hangs in Windsor Castle.

In 1688 James II's Catholic second wife, Mary of Modena, gave birth to a son, giving rise to a genuine fear of a Catholic succession (see page 64 for details of the Bill of Rights of 1689). William of Orange, professing himself Protector of the Protestant cause, was invited to invade Britain, and seized the throne without bloodshed, ruling jointly with his wife, James II's daughter, as William III and Mary II. This joint monarchy was unique in the history of Britain. The Protestant succession was secured by the Act of Settlement of 1701 (see page 64).

Mary II took little part in public affairs and died childless in 1694. William III continued as sole Sovereign until his death in 1702. Anne, Mary II's sister, began her reign in 1702. Tragically, of her many children only one survived infancy, and he died at the age of eleven.

The five eldest children of Charles I, Sir Anthony Van Dyck, 1637

In the absence of an immediate successor, the crown passed to George I, the first of the Hanoverian kings. George I's succession had been achieved by the Act of Settlement of 1701 (see page 64), which regulated the future descent of the Crown to ensure Protestant rule. The settlement declared Electress Sophia of Hanover (niece of Charles I, and granddaughter of James I) heiress presumptive. It was her son George who succeeded as King George I after Queen Anne's death, bypassing Catholic claimants to the throne.

James II's children by his second wife, Mary of Modena, were raised as Catholics but continued to claim the right of succession. James, Prince of Wales, known as 'The Old Pretender', was proclaimed King James III by his Jacobite supporters on the death of James II in 1701; and in 1715 he launched an unsuccessful uprising against George I. A second attempt by his son, 'Bonnie Prince Charlie', in 1745 also failed. The male line of the Stuart family died out in 1807 with the death of Henry, Cardinal York. The heirs to the houses of Normandy (the family of William the Conqueror), Plantagenet, Tudor and Stuart claim their right of succession through Henrietta, the youngest sister of Charles II and James II, though as Catholics they are debarred.

Charles II, c.1661, John Michael Wright. Charles succeeded to the throne in 1660, after the Commonwealth, during which England did not have a monarch.

Mary II, Willem Wissing, mid-1680s

William III, after Sir Godfrey Kneller, 1700. William reigned jointly with his wife, Mary II, until her death in 1694, and then alone until his death in 1702.

RIGHT: *Queen Anne*, Sir Godfrey Kneller, 1710. Anne bore many children, but none survived to adulthood.

House of Stuart

JAMES VI
KING OF SCOTLAND
(1566–1625)
JAMES I
KING OF ENGLAND
r.24 March 1603 – 27 March 1625
(see KINGS AND QUEENS OF SCOTLAND)

= 1590

Anne of Denmark
(1574–1619)
daughter of Frederik II,
King of Denmark & Norway
QUEEN ANNE

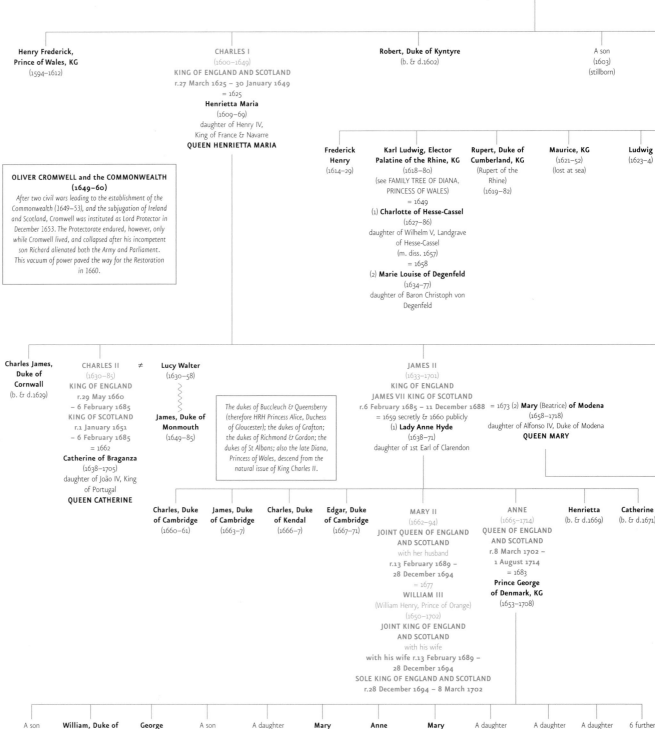

Henry Frederick, Prince of Wales, KG
(1594–1612)

CHARLES I
(1600–1649)
KING OF ENGLAND AND SCOTLAND
r.27 March 1625 – 30 January 1649
= 1625
Henrietta Maria
(1609–69)
daughter of Henry IV,
King of France & Navarre
QUEEN HENRIETTA MARIA

Robert, Duke of Kyntyre
(b. & d.1602)

A son
(1603)
(stillborn)

Frederick Henry
(1614–29)

Karl Ludwig, Elector Palatine of the Rhine, KG
(1618–80)
(see FAMILY TREE OF DIANA, PRINCESS OF WALES)
= 1649
(1) **Charlotte of Hesse-Cassel**
(1627–86)
daughter of Wilhelm V, Landgrave
of Hesse-Cassel
(m. diss. 1657)
= 1658
(2) **Marie Louise of Degenfeld**
(1634–77)
daughter of Baron Christoph von
Degenfeld

Rupert, Duke of Cumberland, KG
(Rupert of the Rhine)
(1619–82)

Maurice, KG
(1621–52)
(lost at sea)

Ludwig
(1623–4)

OLIVER CROMWELL and the COMMONWEALTH (1649–60)

After two civil wars leading to the establishment of the Commonwealth (1649–53), and the subjugation of Ireland and Scotland, Cromwell was instituted as Lord Protector in December 1653. The Protectorate endured, however, only while Cromwell lived, and collapsed after his incompetent son Richard alienated both the Army and Parliament. This vacuum of power paved the way for the Restoration in 1660.

Charles James, Duke of Cornwall
(b. & d.1629)

CHARLES II
(1630–85)
KING OF ENGLAND
r.29 May 1660 – 6 February 1685
KING OF SCOTLAND
r.1 January 1651 – 6 February 1685
= 1662
Catherine of Braganza
(1638–1705)
daughter of João IV, King
of Portugal
QUEEN CATHERINE

≠

Lucy Walter
(1630–58)

James, Duke of Monmouth
(1649–85)

The dukes of Buccleuch & Queensberry (therefore HRH Princess Alice, Duchess of Gloucester); the dukes of Grafton; the dukes of Richmond & Gordon; the dukes of St Albans; also the late Diana, Princess of Wales, descend from the natural issue of King Charles II.

JAMES II
(1633–1701)
KING OF ENGLAND
JAMES VII KING OF SCOTLAND
r.6 February 1685 – 11 December 1688
= 1659 secretly & 1660 publicly
(1) **Lady Anne Hyde**
(1638–71)
daughter of 1st Earl of Clarendon

= 1673 (2) **Mary** (Beatrice) **of Modena**
(1658–1718)
daughter of Alfonso IV, Duke of Modena
QUEEN MARY

Charles, Duke of Cambridge
(1660–61)

James, Duke of Cambridge
(1663–7)

Charles, Duke of Kendal
(1666–7)

Edgar, Duke of Cambridge
(1667–71)

MARY II
(1662–94)
JOINT QUEEN OF ENGLAND AND SCOTLAND
with her husband
r.13 February 1689 – 28 December 1694
= 1677
WILLIAM III
(William Henry, Prince of Orange)
(1650–1702)
JOINT KING OF ENGLAND AND SCOTLAND
with his wife
with his wife r.13 February 1689 – 28 December 1694
SOLE KING OF ENGLAND AND SCOTLAND
r.28 December 1694 – 8 March 1702

ANNE
(1665–1714)
QUEEN OF ENGLAND AND SCOTLAND
r.8 March 1702 – 1 August 1714
= 1683
Prince George of Denmark, KG
(1653–1708)

Henrietta
(b. & d.1669)

Catherine
(b. & d.1671)

A son
(1687)
(stillborn)

William, Duke of Gloucester, KG
(1689–1700)

George
(b. & d.1696)

A son
(1698)
(stillborn)

A daughter
(1684)
(stillborn)

Mary
(1685–7)

Anne
(1686–7)

Mary
(b. & d.1690)

A daughter
(1693)
(stillborn)

A daughter
(1696)
(stillborn)

A daughter
(1700)
(stillborn)

6 further miscarried or stillborn children

Arms of KING CHARLES I

Arms of KING WILLIAM III

Arms of QUEEN ANNE

Elizabeth
(1596–1662)
= 1613
Frederick V
(1596–1632)
King of Bohemia
and Elector Palatine of the Rhine

Margaret
(1598–1600)

Mary
(1605–7)

Sophia
(b. & d.1606)

Edward, KG
(1624–63)
= 1645
Anne
(1616–84)
ghter of Charles, Duke of
Nevers & Mantua
rced wife of Duc de Guise)

Philip
(1627–50)
(killed at Battle of
Rethel)

Gustavus
(1632–41)

Elizabeth
(1618–80)

Louise
(1622–1709)

Henrietta Maria
(1626–51)
= 1651
Sigismund Rákóczy,
Prince of
Siebenbürgen
(d.1652)

Charlotte
(1628–31)

SOPHIA
(1630–1714)
Heiress presumptive
1702–14
= 1658
Ernst August, Elector of Hanover & Duke
of Brunswick-Lüneburg & Zelle, KG
(1629–98)

GEORGE I
(1660–1727)
KING OF GREAT BRITAIN
(see FAMILY OF GEORGE I AND
GEORGE II)

Friedrich August
(1661–91)
(killed in battle)

Maximilian
(1666–1726)

A son
(1666)
(stillborn twin with
Maximilian)

Karl Philip
(1669–90)
(killed in battle)

Christian
(1671–1703)
(drowned in the
Danube)

Ernst August,
Duke of York &
Albany, KG
(1674–1728)

Sophie Charlotte
(1668–1705)
= 1684
Frederick I
(1657–1713)
King in Prussia, KG
as his second wife

Friedrich Wilhelm I
(1688–1740)
King in Prussia, KG
(1706)
=
Sophia Dorothea
(1687–1757)
daughter of King George I

Henry, Duke of
Gloucester, KG
(1640–60)

Mary
(1631–60)
(The Princess Royal)
= 1641
Willem II, Prince of
Orange
(d.1650)

William Henry,
Prince of Orange
(1650–1702)
KING WILLIAM III,
JOINT KING OF
ENGLAND AND
SCOTLAND

Elizabeth
(1635–50)

Anne
(1637–40)

Catherine
(b. & d.1639)

Henrietta
(1644–70)
= 1661
Philippe, Duke of
Orleans
(1640–1701)

Descendants of Philippe, Duke of Orleans, being Roman Catholics are excluded from the succession. The present representative is Franz, Duke of Bavaria (b.1933).

harles, Duke of
Cambridge
(b. & d.1677)

James, Prince of
Wales, KG
(1688–1766)
(The Old Pretender,
proclaimed
King James III in 1701)
= 1719
Clementina Sobieska
(1702–35)
daughter of Prince
Jakob Sobieski, son of
Jan III, King of Poland

Catherine
(b. & d.1675)

Isabella
(1676–81)

Charlotte
(b. & d.1682)

Louisa
(1692–1712)

Charles Edward
(1720–88)
nce of Wales; Prince Regent in Scotland 1745;
Count of Albany; 'The Young Pretender',
recognized as Charles III by his adherents)
= 1772
Princess Louise of Stolberg-Gedern
(1752–1824)
ughter of Gustavus, Prince of Stolberg-Gedern

Henry Benedict,
Duke of York,
Cardinal York
(1725–1807)
recognised as Henry
IX by his adherents

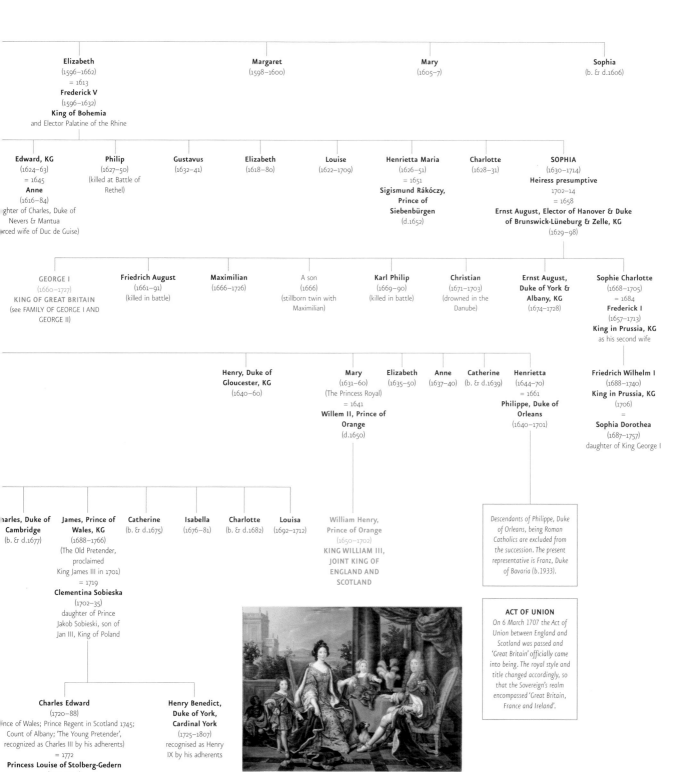

The family of James II, Pierre Mignard, 1694

ACT OF UNION

On 6 March 1707 the Act of Union between England and Scotland was passed and 'Great Britain' officially came into being. The royal style and title changed accordingly, so that the Sovereign's realm encompassed 'Great Britain, France and Ireland'.

Families of George I, George II and George III

THE HOUSE OF HANOVER LEADS IN DIRECT AND UNBROKEN SUCCESSION FROM GEORGE LOUIS, ELECTOR OF HANOVER, WHO SUCCEEDED QUEEN ANNE IN 1714, TO QUEEN ELIZABETH II.

George Louis succeeded to the throne as King George I in 1714 under the terms of the Act of Settlement of 1701 (see pages 34 and 64). Hanover (which became a kingdom in 1814) was thus joined to the British Crown and remained so until 1837. Queen Victoria was unable to inherit the Kingdom of Hanover because, under the semi-Salic law that applied there, a woman could not inherit if there was a male heir. It passed instead to her uncle, the Duke of Cumberland. George I arrived in Britain in 1714, having divorced his wife for adultery in 1694. He never learned to speak English, was neither a popular nor an able king, and was in constant dispute with his son, the Prince of Wales. In 1727 he died at Osnabrück.

George I was succeeded by George II, who was born in Hanover. A more popular sovereign than his father, he was soundly advised by his wife, Caroline of Brandenburg-Ansbach, who played a greater role in affairs of state than most queens consort. George II's reign was largely peaceful, despite the second Jacobite Uprising of 1745 led by Charles, the Young Pretender ('Bonnie Prince Charlie'), grandson of James II.

George II's son, Frederick, Prince of Wales, died suddenly in 1751, so George II was succeeded by Frederick's son, as George III.

George III was the first British-born king in the House of Hanover. His 60-year reign saw both the American War of

George I, John Vanderbank, 1726. The first King of the House of Hanover.

George II, John Shackleton, 1760–65. The second King of the House of Hanover.

FAR LEFT:
George III, Allan Ramsay, 1761–2. The King is in his Coronation robes.

LEFT:
George IV when Prince of Wales, Sir William Beechey, 1803

Independence (as a result of which Britain lost her colonies in America) and the Napoleonic Wars in Europe. George III was plagued by attacks of mental illness, now known to be porphyria. As a result, his son the Prince of Wales served as Regent from 1811 until George III's death in 1820.

The Prince Regent succeeded as George IV, and reigned until 1830. He was an extravagant and extrovert figure, who converted Buckingham House into a stately palace, built the Royal Pavilion at Brighton, created Carlton House in London and remodelled Windsor Castle. The Royal Marriages Act (see page 64), passed during his father's reign, affected the new king. His marriage in 1785 to the twice-widowed Roman Catholic Mary Anne Fitzherbert had been declared null and void, and he was obliged to marry his cousin Caroline of Brunswick in 1795. This marriage was controversial and unsatisfactory (he even debarred his wife from the Coronation), although it produced a daughter, Charlotte, in 1796. Charlotte married Prince Leopold of Saxe-Coburg-Saalfeld, but died in childbirth in 1817.

On Charlotte's death, the Prince Regent's surviving six brothers and five sisters were left in the line of succession to the throne. Two of the royal dukes were married without legitimate children, three were unmarried, while one had been married in contravention of the Royal Marriages Act. This situation created much concern and thus, within about two months of each other in 1818, the three bachelor princes married. One of them, the Duke of Kent, gained an heir, the future Queen Victoria, in 1819.

The second son of George III was Frederick, Duke of York, who died childless in 1827. George IV was therefore succeeded by his next brother, William IV, who reigned from 1830 to 1837. William IV had two legitimate daughters, who both died young.

George III's family tree also contains many of the descendants of Adolphus, Duke of Cambridge (1774–1850). Adolphus had a son and two daughters, the younger of whom, Mary Adelaide, was married to the Duke of Teck, and was the mother of Princess Victoria Mary (Princess May). Princess May was engaged to the Duke of Clarence, the second in direct line of succession to Queen Victoria, in 1891. After the Duke of Clarence died early the following year, Princess May married the new heir, George, Duke of York; they became King George V and Queen Mary. Thus Queen Elizabeth II has dual descent from George III, through the Duke of Kent and the Duke of Cambridge.

Arms of GEORGE I and II

GEORGE II
(1683–1760)
KING OF GREAT BRITAIN AND IRELAND
r.11 June 1727 – 25 October 1760
= 1705
Princess Caroline of Brandenburg-Ansbach
(1683–1737)
daughter of Johann Friedrich, Margrave of Brandenburg-Ansbach
QUEEN CAROLINE

Frederick, Prince of Wales, KG
(1707–51)
= 1736
Princess Augusta of Saxe-Gotha-Altenburg
(1719–72)
daughter of HSH Friedrich II, Duke of Saxe-Gotha-Altenburg

A son
(stillborn, 1716)

GEORGE III
(1738–1820)
KING OF GREAT BRITAIN AND IRELAND (THE UNITED KINGDOM)
(see FAMILY OF KING GEORGE III)

Edward, Duke of York & Albany, KG
(1739–67)

The family of George II, William Hogarth , 1731–2

George III, Queen Charlotte and their six eldest children, Johan Zoffany, 1770

Family of George I and George II

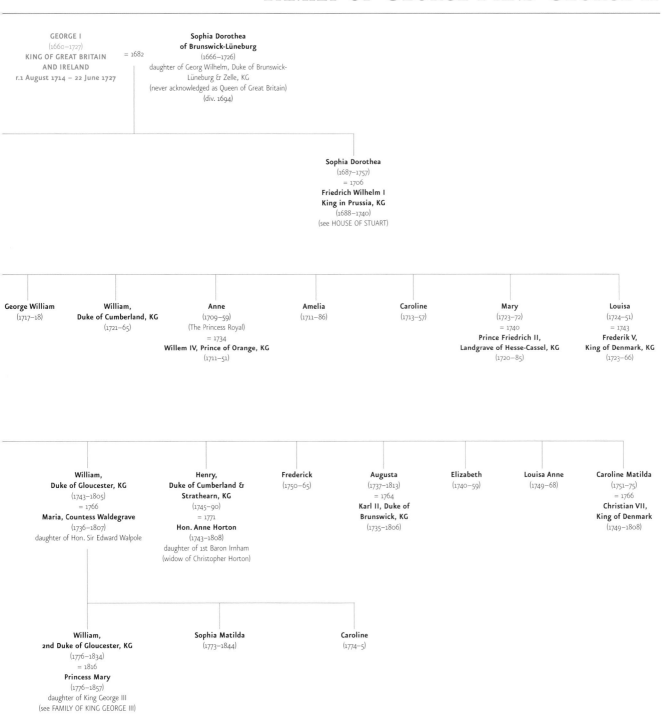

GEORGE I
(1660–1727)
KING OF GREAT BRITAIN AND IRELAND
r.1 August 1714 – 22 June 1727

= 1682

Sophia Dorothea of Brunswick-Lüneburg
(1666–1726)
daughter of Georg Wilhelm, Duke of Brunswick-Lüneburg & Zelle, KG
(never acknowledged as Queen of Great Britain)
(div. 1694)

Sophia Dorothea
(1687–1757)
= 1706
Friedrich Wilhelm I King in Prussia, KG
(1688–1740)
(see HOUSE OF STUART)

George William
(1717–18)

William, Duke of Cumberland, KG
(1721–65)

Anne
(1709–59)
(The Princess Royal)
= 1734
Willem IV, Prince of Orange, KG
(1711–51)

Amelia
(1711–86)

Caroline
(1713–57)

Mary
(1723–72)
= 1740
Prince Friedrich II, Landgrave of Hesse-Cassel, KG
(1720–85)

Louisa
(1724–51)
= 1743
Frederik V, King of Denmark, KG
(1723–66)

William, Duke of Gloucester, KG
(1743–1805)
= 1766
Maria, Countess Waldegrave
(1736–1807)
daughter of Hon. Sir Edward Walpole

Henry, Duke of Cumberland & Strathearn, KG
(1745–90)
= 1771
Hon. Anne Horton
(1743–1808)
daughter of 1st Baron Irnham
(widow of Christopher Horton)

Frederick
(1750–65)

Augusta
(1737–1813)
= 1764
Karl II, Duke of Brunswick, KG
(1735–1806)

Elizabeth
(1740–59)

Louisa Anne
(1749–68)

Caroline Matilda
(1751–75)
= 1766
Christian VII, King of Denmark
(1749–1808)

William, 2nd Duke of Gloucester, KG
(1776–1834)
= 1816
Princess Mary
(1776–1857)
daughter of King George III
(see FAMILY OF KING GEORGE III)

Sophia Matilda
(1773–1844)

Caroline
(1774–5)

Family of King George III

GEORGE III
(1738–1820)
KING OF THE UNITED KINGDOM OF GREAT BRITAIN AND NORTHERN IRELAND
r.25 October 1760 – 29 January 1820

= 1761

Princess Charlotte of Mecklenburg-Strelitz
(1744–1818)
daughter of Duke Karl of Mecklenburg-Strelitz
QUEEN CHARLOTTE

GEORGE IV
(1762–1830)
KING OF THE UNITED KINGDOM OF GREAT BRITAIN AND NORTHERN IRELAND
Regent from 5 February 1811
r.29 January 1820 – 26 June 1830
= 1785
(1) **Mrs Mary Anne Fitzherbert** (1756–1837)
daughter of Walter Smythe
(in contravention of the Royal Marriages Act; marriage declared null and void)
= 1795
(2) **Princess Caroline of Brunswick**
(1768–1821)
(his 1st cousin)
daughter of Karl II, Duke of Brunswick, KG

Charlotte of Wales Heiress Presumptive
(1796–1817)
= 1816
Prince Leopold of Saxe-Coburg-Saalfeld, KG
(1790–1865)
(later Leopold I, King of the Belgians)

A son
(1817)
(stillborn)

Frederick, Duke of York & Albany, KG
(1763–1827)
= 1791
Princess Frederica of Prussia
(1767–1820)
daughter of King Friedrich Wilhelm II of Prussia

WILLIAM IV
(1765–1837)
KING OF THE UNITED KINGDOM OF GREAT BRITAIN AND NORTHERN IRELAND
r.26 June 1830 – 20 June 1837
= 1818
Princess Adelaide of Saxe-Meiningen
(1792–1849)
daughter of Duke Georg I of Saxe-Meiningen
QUEEN ADELAIDE

Charlotte
(b. & d.1819)

Elizabeth
(1820–21)

Edward, Duke of Kent, KG
(1767–1820)
= 1818
Princess Victoria
(1786–1861)
The Duchess of Kent
daughter of Prince Franz, Duke of Saxe-Coburg-Saalfeld
(widow of Prince Emich Karl of Leiningen)

ALEXANDRINA VICTORIA
(1819–1901)
QUEEN VICTORIA
QUEEN OF THE UNITED KINGDOM OF GREAT BRITAIN AND NORTHERN IRELAND,
EMPRESS OF INDIA
(see FAMILY OF QUEEN VICTORIA)

Ernest Augustus, Duke of Cumberland, KG
(1771–1851)
(Ernst August, King of Hanover from 1837)
= 1815
Princess Frederica
(1778–1841)
daughter of Prince Karl, Duke of Mecklenburg-Strelitz
(widow of Prince Friedrich of Solms-Braunfels, & of Prince Ludwig of Prussia)

Georg V, King of Hanover, KG
(1819–78)
(lost throne of Hanover to Prussia, 1866)
= 1843
Princess Marie of Saxe-Altenburg
(1818–1907)
daughter of Duke Joseph of Saxe-Altenburg

Ernst August, Crown Prince of Hanover, 3rd Duke of Cumberland
(1845–1923)
= 1878
Princess Thyra of Denmark
(1853–1933)
daughter of King Christian IX of Denmark, KG

from whom descend the present royal House of Hanover, and the royal family of Greece

Frederica
(1848–1926)
= 1880
Baron Alfons von Pawel-Rammingen
(1843–1932)

Victoria von Pawel-Rammingen
(b. & d.1881)

Marie
(1849–1904)

George, 2nd Marquess of Cambridge
(1895–1981)
= 1923
Dorothy Hastings
(1899–1988)
(Marchioness of Cambridge)
daughter of Hon. Osmond Hastings

Lady Mary Cambridge
(1924–1999)
=
Peter Whitley
(1923–2003)

King George IV, Sir Thomas Lawrence, 1821

Arms of KING GEORGE III

Augustus,
Duke of Sussex, KG
(1773–1843)
= 1793 (1) **Lady Augusta Murray**
(1768–1830)
daughter of 4th Earl of Dunmore
(m. annulled 1794)
= 1831 (2) **Lady Cecilia Underwood,**
Duchess of Inverness
(1785–1873)
daughter of 2nd Earl of Arran
(both in contravention of the Royal Marriages Act)

Adolphus,
Duke of Cambridge, KG
(1774–1850)
= 1818
Princess Augusta of Hesse-Cassel
(1797–1889)
daughter of Prince Friedrich of Hesse-Cassel

Octavius
(1779–83)

Alfred
(1780–82)

Charlotte
(1766–1828)
(The Princess Royal)
= 1797
King Friedrich I of Württemberg
(1754–1816)

Augusta
(1768–1840)

Elizabeth
(1770–1840)
= 1818
Friedrich VI, Landgrave of Hesse-Homburg
(1769–1829)

Mary
(1776–1857)
(Duchess of Gloucester)
= 1816
Prince William, 2nd Duke of Gloucester, KG
(1776–1834)
(see FAMILY OF GEORGE I AND GEORGE II)

Sophia
(1777–1848)

Amelia
(1783–1810)

George,
Duke of Cambridge, KG
(1819–1904)
= 1847
Sarah (Louisa) Fairbrother (Mrs Fitzgeorge)
(1816–90)
daughter of Robert Fairbrother
(in contravention of the Royal Marriages Act)

Augusta
(1822–1916)
= 1843
Grand Duke Friedrich Wilhelm of Mecklenburg-Strelitz, KG
(1819–1904)

Mary Adelaide
(1833–97)
= 1866
Prince Francis, Duke of Teck
(1837–1900)

Adolphus,
1st Marquess of Cambridge
(1868–1927)
= 1894
Lady Margaret Grosvenor
(1873–1929)
daughter of 1st Duke of Westminster, KG

Prince Francis of Teck
(1870–1910)

Prince Alexander of Teck
(1874–1957)
(1st Earl of Athlone, KG)
= 1904
Princess Alice of Albany
(1883–1981)
(Princess Alice, Countess of Athlone)
(see FAMILY OF QUEEN VICTORIA)

Princess Victoria Mary of Teck
(1867–1953)
QUEEN MARY
= 1893
GEORGE V
(1865–1936)
KING OF THE UNITED KINGDOM OF GREAT BRITAIN AND NORTHERN IRELAND, EMPEROR OF INDIA
(see HOUSE OF WINDSOR)

Frederick
(Lord Frederick Cambridge)
(1907–40)
ed in action in France)

Mary
(1897–1987)
(Mary, Duchess of Beaufort)
= 1923
Henry, 10th Duke of Beaufort, KG
(1900–1984)

Helena
(1899–1969)
(Lady Helena Gibbs)
= 1919
Colonel John Evelyn Gibbs
(1879–1932)

Rupert, Viscount Trematon
(1907–28)

Maurice
(b. & d.1910)

May
(1906–94)
(Lady May Abel Smith)
= 1931
Colonel Sir Henry Abel Smith
(1900–1993)

descendants

William IV, Sir David Wilkie, 1832. The 'Sailor King' is shown here in his Garter robes.

Family of Queen Victoria

QUEEN VICTORIA SUCCEEDED TO THE THRONE IN 1837, AND REIGNED FOR SIXTY-THREE YEARS. DURING HER LONG REIGN, SHE ESTABLISHED HERSELF AS A HIGHLY RESPECTED MONARCH, VERY DIFFERENT FROM HER HANOVERIAN FOREBEARS. HER MARRIAGE TO PRINCE ALBERT OF SAXE-COBURG AND GOTHA BROUGHT HIS POWERFUL INFLUENCE TO THE COURT.

Prince Albert's death in 1861 left the Queen bereft; during the middle years of her reign she was seldom seen in public. Victoria became Empress of India in 1877, and by the time of her Golden Jubilee in 1887 and her Diamond Jubilee in 1897 she had become a much-revered monarch at the centre of a huge Empire.

Prince Albert predeceased his childless elder brother (Ernst II, Duke of Coburg), which meant that one of his and Queen Victoria's sons would have to succeed their uncle in Coburg. The Prince of Wales renounced his claim to the duchy and the succession passed to his next brother, Alfred, Duke of Edinburgh, who became Duke of Saxe-Coburg and Gotha in 1893. His son, Alfred, predeceased him, and in 1900 the next heir was Arthur, Duke of Connaught, followed by his son, Prince Arthur of Connaught. Both father and son made it clear that they did not wish to reside in Coburg; they were strongly supported by Queen Victoria, and the Coburg succession passed to the son of Prince Leopold, Duke of Albany, who had died in 1884. His son, Prince Charles Edward, 2nd Duke of Albany,

LEFT:
Queen Victoria, Sir George Hayter, 1838. The Queen is depicted in her Coronation robes.

RIGHT:
Queen Victoria, Heinrich von Angeli, 1899. Shown in old age, the Queen reigned for over 63 years.

ABOVE: *The Royal Family in 1846*, Franz Xaver Winterhalter. The painting shows Queen Victoria and Prince Albert (The Prince Consort) with their elder children, Alfred, Duke of Edinburgh, Albert Edward, Prince of Wales (later King Edward VII), Alice, Grand Duchess of Hesse, Princess Helena and Victoria (the future Empress Frederick of Germany).

OPPOSITE: *The family of Queen Victoria in 1887*, by Laurits Regner Tuxen. Painted at Windsor Castle. Queen Victoria is surrounded by her descendants and their spouses, at the time of the Golden Jubilee in 1887. The little girl in the centre foreground was the last surviving grandchild of the Queen – Princess Alice, Countess of Athlone, who lived to the age of 97, dying in 1981.

became Duke of Saxe-Coburg and Gotha. He found himself on the 'enemy' side in the First World War, and was eventually stripped of his English dukedom and subsidiary titles. In 1915 he was also struck from the roll of the Order of the Garter. Before the Second World War he became involved with the Nazi party, and was imprisoned at the end of the war. He died a broken man in 1954.

But for the Coburg succession, Charles Edward's descendants might have been brought up in England and served as minor members of the British royal family. As it is, his daughter, Sibylla, was the mother of the present King of Sweden. Many European royal families descend from Queen Victoria, including those of Sweden, Denmark, Norway and Spain, and the erstwhile royal houses of Germany, Russia, Greece and Romania. The Kaiser was the son of Queen Victoria's eldest daughter, Victoria, Empress Frederick.

The family tree of Queen Victoria does not show the descendants of King Edward VII (see tree for the House of Saxe-Coburg and Gotha, page 49), nor those of Alice, Grand Duchess of Hesse, from whom Prince Philip, Duke of Edinburgh, descends (see tree for the Ancestry of HRH The Duke of Edinburgh, page 56).

Family of Queen Victoria

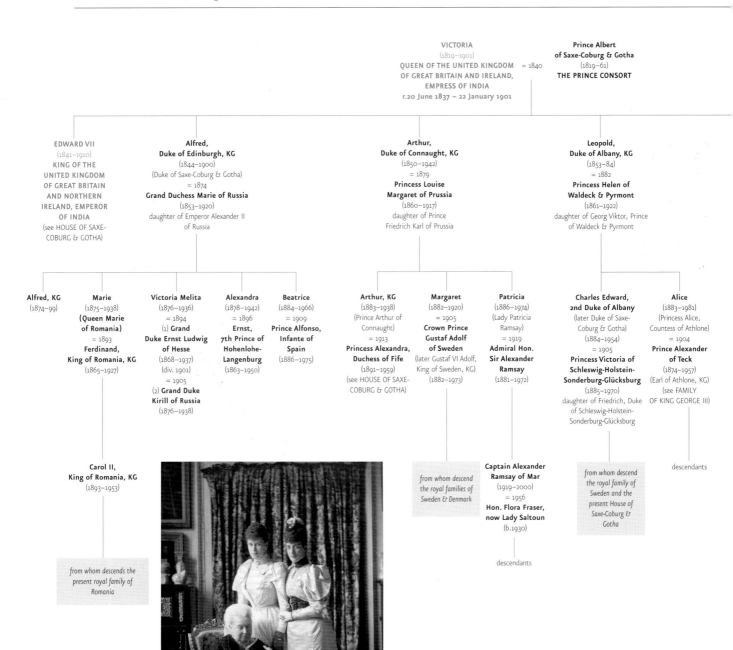

VICTORIA (1819–1901) QUEEN OF THE UNITED KINGDOM OF GREAT BRITAIN AND IRELAND, EMPRESS OF INDIA r.20 June 1837 – 22 January 1901 = 1840 **Prince Albert of Saxe-Coburg & Gotha** (1819–61) **THE PRINCE CONSORT**

- EDWARD VII (1841–1910) KING OF THE UNITED KINGDOM OF GREAT BRITAIN AND NORTHERN IRELAND, EMPEROR OF INDIA (see HOUSE OF SAXE-COBURG & GOTHA)
- **Alfred, Duke of Edinburgh, KG** (1844–1900) (Duke of Saxe-Coburg & Gotha) = 1874 **Grand Duchess Marie of Russia** (1853–1920) daughter of Emperor Alexander II of Russia
  - **Alfred, KG** (1874–99)
  - **Marie** (1875–1938) **(Queen Marie of Romania)** = 1893 **Ferdinand, King of Romania, KG** (1865–1927)
    - **Carol II, King of Romania, KG** (1893–1953)
      - *from whom descends the present royal family of Romania*
  - **Victoria Melita** (1876–1936) = 1894 (1) **Grand Duke Ernst Ludwig of Hesse** (1868–1937) (div. 1901) = 1905 (2) **Grand Duke Kirill of Russia** (1876–1938)
  - **Alexandra** (1878–1942) = 1896 **Ernst, 7th Prince of Hohenlohe-Langenburg** (1863–1950)
  - **Beatrice** (1884–1966) = 1909 **Prince Alfonso, Infante of Spain** (1886–1975)
- **Arthur, Duke of Connaught, KG** (1850–1942) = 1879 **Princess Louise Margaret of Prussia** (1860–1917) daughter of Prince Friedrich Karl of Prussia
  - **Arthur, KG** (1883–1938) (Prince Arthur of Connaught) = 1913 **Princess Alexandra, Duchess of Fife** (1891–1959) (see HOUSE OF SAXE-COBURG & GOTHA)
  - **Margaret** (1882–1920) = 1905 **Crown Prince Gustaf Adolf of Sweden** (later Gustaf VI Adolf, King of Sweden, KG) (1882–1973)
    - *from whom descend the royal families of Sweden & Denmark*
  - **Patricia** (1886–1974) (Lady Patricia Ramsay) = 1919 **Admiral Hon. Sir Alexander Ramsay** (1881–1972)
    - **Captain Alexander Ramsay of Mar** (1919–2000) = 1956 **Hon. Flora Fraser, now Lady Saltoun** (b.1930)
      - descendants
- **Leopold, Duke of Albany, KG** (1853–84) = 1882 **Princess Helen of Waldeck & Pyrmont** (1861–1922) daughter of Georg Viktor, Prince of Waldeck & Pyrmont
  - **Charles Edward, 2nd Duke of Albany** (later Duke of Saxe-Coburg & Gotha) (1884–1954) = 1905 **Princess Victoria of Schleswig-Holstein-Sonderburg-Glücksburg** (1885–1970) daughter of Friedrich, Duke of Schleswig-Holstein-Sonderburg-Glücksburg
    - *from whom descend the royal family of Sweden and the present House of Saxe-Coburg & Gotha*
  - **Alice** (1883–1981) (Princess Alice, Countess of Athlone) = 1904 **Prince Alexander of Teck** (1874–1957) (Earl of Athlone, KG) (see FAMILY OF KING GEORGE III)
    - descendants

Queen Victoria holds her great-grandson, Prince Edward of York, at his Christening on 16 July 1894. Standing behind are Alexandra, Princess of Wales, the Prince's grandmother; and his mother, Victoria Mary, Duchess of York.

Arms of QUEEN VICTORIA

Arms of PRINCE ALBERT, THE PRINCE CONSORT

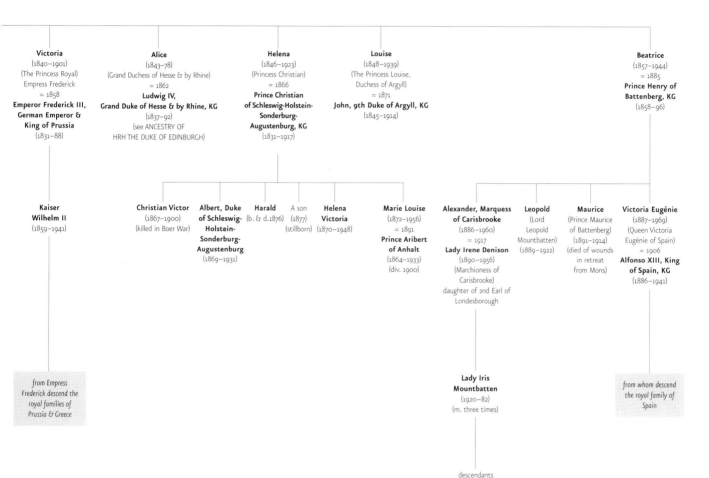

Victoria
(1840–1901)
(The Princess Royal)
Empress Frederick
= 1858
Emperor Frederick III, German Emperor & King of Prussia
(1831–88)

Kaiser Wilhelm II
(1859–1941)

from Empress Frederick descend the royal families of Prussia & Greece

Alice
(1843–78)
(Grand Duchess of Hesse & by Rhine)
= 1862
Ludwig IV, Grand Duke of Hesse & by Rhine, KG
(1837–92)
(see ANCESTRY OF HRH THE DUKE OF EDINBURGH)

Helena
(1846–1923)
(Princess Christian)
= 1866
Prince Christian of Schleswig-Holstein-Sonderburg-Augustenburg, KG
(1831–1917)

Christian Victor
(1867–1900)
(killed in Boer War)

Albert, Duke of Schleswig-Holstein-Sonderburg-Augustenburg
(1869–1931)

Harald
(b. & d.1876)

A son
(1877)
(stillborn)

Helena Victoria
(1870–1948)

Marie Louise
(1872–1956)
= 1891
Prince Aribert of Anhalt
(1864–1933)
(div. 1900)

Louise
(1848–1939)
(The Princess Louise, Duchess of Argyll)
= 1871
John, 9th Duke of Argyll, KG
(1845–1914)

Beatrice
(1857–1944)
= 1885
Prince Henry of Battenberg, KG
(1858–96)

Alexander, Marquess of Carisbrooke
(1886–1960)
= 1917
Lady Irene Denison
(1890–1956)
(Marchioness of Carisbrooke)
daughter of 2nd Earl of Londesborough

Lady Iris Mountbatten
(1920–82)
(m. three times)

descendants

Leopold
(Lord Leopold Mountbatten)
(1889–1922)

Maurice
(Prince Maurice of Battenberg)
(1891–1914)
(died of wounds in retreat from Mons)

Victoria Eugénie
(1887–1969)
(Queen Victoria Eugénie of Spain)
= 1906
Alfonso XIII, King of Spain, KG
(1886–1941)

from whom descend the royal family of Spain

Queen Victoria, Prince Albert, and seven of their children photographed in the garden at Buckingham Palace by Roger Fenton, 22 May 1854 (detail).

House of Saxe-Coburg and Gotha

IN 1901 KING EDWARD VII BECAME THE FIRST KING OF THE HOUSE OF SAXE-COBURG AND GOTHA, THE FAMILY NAME OF HIS FATHER, PRINCE ALBERT, THE PRINCE CONSORT.

For his first sixty years, as Prince of Wales he had been prevented from participating in affairs of state. Although he undertook an increasing number of official duties, he was widely perceived as being indolent and pleasure-loving. Yet when he became King at the age of fifty-nine, he proved extremely popular with his subjects. His skill for diplomacy and foreign affairs helped to achieve the Entente Cordiale in 1904 with France.

In 1863 the future King Edward VII had married Princess Alexandra of Denmark. They had three sons and three daughters. Their eldest son, Albert Victor, Duke of Clarence, died unmarried in 1892, so the succession passed to the Duke of York, who succeeded to the throne as King George V in 1910.

King Edward VII's eldest daughter, Princess Louise, married the Duke of Fife and had two daughters, Princesses Alexandra and Maud. Alistair, the Duke of Connaught, the heir to Princess Alexandra (Princess Arthur of Connaught, Duchess of Fife in her own right), died in 1943. Princess Maud had married Lord Carnegie, later Earl of Southesk. She died before Alexandra, and the Dukedom of Fife passed to her son, the present Duke of Fife (b.1929).

King Edward VII's youngest daughter, Maud, married Prince Charles of Denmark, who was elected King of Norway in 1905 and took the name of Haakon VII. Their son, Olav V (1903–91), was a regular visitor to Britain, and his descendants include the present King of Norway, Harald V. King Edward's second daughter, Princess Victoria, remained unmarried.

Albert Victor, Duke of Clarence & Avondale, KG
(1864–92)

GEORGE V
(1865–1936)
KING OF THE UNITED KING
GREAT BRITAIN AND NORT
IRELAND, EMPEROR OF I
(see HOUSE OF WINDSO

A son
(1890)
(stillborn)

Alexandra, Duchess of Fife
(1891–1959)
(known as Princess Arthu
of Connaught)
= 1913
Prince Arthur of Connaught, KG
(1883–1938)

Alastair, 2nd Duke of Connaught
(1914–43)

The Coronation of King Edward VII, Edwin Austin Abbey, 1902–7. The King is shown at the moment of crowning by Frederick Temple, the Archbishop of Canterbury. Queen Alexandra is in front of the royal box in the background.

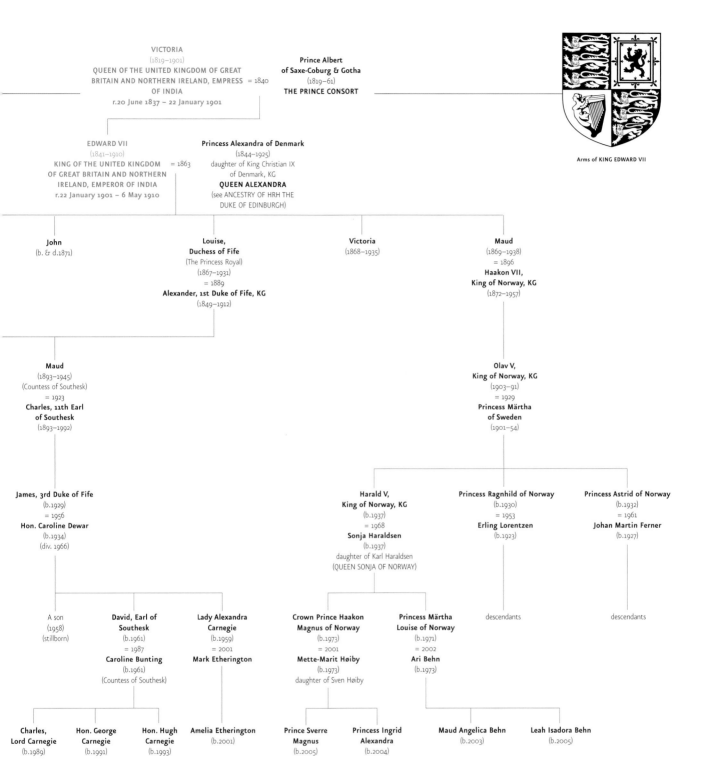

VICTORIA
(1819–1901)
QUEEN OF THE UNITED KINGDOM OF GREAT BRITAIN AND NORTHERN IRELAND, EMPRESS OF INDIA
r.20 June 1837 – 22 January 1901

= 1840

Prince Albert of Saxe-Coburg & Gotha
(1819–61)
THE PRINCE CONSORT

Arms of KING EDWARD VII

EDWARD VII
(1841–1910)
KING OF THE UNITED KINGDOM OF GREAT BRITAIN AND NORTHERN IRELAND, EMPEROR OF INDIA
r.22 January 1901 – 6 May 1910

= 1863

Princess Alexandra of Denmark
(1844–1925)
daughter of King Christian IX of Denmark, KG
QUEEN ALEXANDRA
(see ANCESTRY OF HRH THE DUKE OF EDINBURGH)

John
(b. & d.1871)

Louise, Duchess of Fife
(The Princess Royal)
(1867–1931)
= 1889
Alexander, 1st Duke of Fife, KG
(1849–1912)

Victoria
(1868–1935)

Maud
(1869–1938)
= 1896
Haakon VII, King of Norway, KG
(1872–1957)

Maud
(1893–1945)
(Countess of Southesk)
= 1923
Charles, 11th Earl of Southesk
(1893–1992)

Olav V, King of Norway, KG
(1903–91)
= 1929
Princess Märtha of Sweden
(1901–54)

James, 3rd Duke of Fife
(b.1929)
= 1956
Hon. Caroline Dewar
(b.1934)
(div. 1966)

Harald V, King of Norway, KG
(b.1937)
= 1968
Sonja Haraldsen
(b.1937)
daughter of Karl Haraldsen
(QUEEN SONJA OF NORWAY)

Princess Ragnhild of Norway
(b.1930)
= 1953
Erling Lorentzen
(b.1923)

Princess Astrid of Norway
(b.1932)
= 1961
Johan Martin Ferner
(b.1927)

A son
(1958)
(stillborn)

David, Earl of Southesk
(b.1961)
= 1987
Caroline Bunting
(b.1961)
(Countess of Southesk)

Lady Alexandra Carnegie
(b.1959)
= 2001
Mark Etherington

Crown Prince Haakon Magnus of Norway
(b.1973)
= 2001
Mette-Marit Høiby
(b.1973)
daughter of Sven Høiby

Princess Märtha Louise of Norway
(b.1971)
= 2002
Ari Behn
(b.1973)

descendants

descendants

Charles, Lord Carnegie
(b.1989)

Hon. George Carnegie
(b.1991)

Hon. Hugh Carnegie
(b.1993)

Amelia Etherington
(b.2001)

Prince Sverre Magnus
(b.2005)

Princess Ingrid Alexandra
(b.2004)

Maud Angelica Behn
(b.2003)

Leah Isadora Behn
(b.2005)

House of Windsor

KING GEORGE V MARRIED PRINCESS VICTORIA MARY (MAY) OF TECK, WHO WAS A DESCENDANT OF GEORGE III THROUGH HER MOTHER, PRINCESS MARY ADELAIDE, DAUGHTER OF ADOLPHUS, DUKE OF CAMBRIDGE.

King George V, Frederick Elwell, 1932. King George V was the first Sovereign of the House of Windsor. The King wears the robes of the Order of the Thistle.

King George V's reign witnessed a number of constitutional crises and the trauma of the First World War. It was as the result of anti-German feelings towards members of the Royal House that King George V dropped the German style of the House of Saxe-Coburg (or Wettin, as the family name was sometimes known). He declared by royal proclamation on 17 July 1917 that 'Our House and Family shall be styled and known as the House and Family of Windsor.' Subsequently it was stated that 'the titles of Prince and Princess will be confined to the children and grandchildren of the Sovereign. The titles of Highness and Serene Highness will be allowed to die out and the use of "Royal Highness" will be confined to the children of the Sovereign and the children of the Sovereign's sons.' It added that 'in the third generation in the male line the younger sons will assume the family name of "Windsor" with the courtesy title of "Younger Sons of a Duke".'

Simultaneously, a number of relatives relinquished their German titles and assumed English ones. Queen Mary's oldest brother, the Duke of Teck, became the Marquess of Cambridge, while her youngest brother became the Earl of Athlone. The daughters of Princess Christian dropped the style 'of Schleswig-Holstein', and the Battenberg descendants of Princesses Beatrice and Alice took the surname of Mountbatten; Prince Louis of Battenberg became the Marquess of Milford Haven, and Princess Beatrice's son, Alexander of Battenberg, became Marquess of Carisbrooke.

The direct effect of the King's proclamation was that the sons of his daughter, Princess Mary, would receive no title from their mother whereas the daughters of Princess Louise, King Edward VII's eldest daughter, had been given titles in their own right.

This arrangement continued until 1952, when Queen Elizabeth II came to the throne. In the normal course of the succession the style of Windsor would have had to change to that of the royal consort. The Earl Mountbatten of Burma – Prince Philip's uncle – assumed that the House of Mountbatten now ruled in Britain. This did not appeal either to Queen Mary or to the Prime Minister, Winston Churchill, who prevailed upon The Queen to declare, in April 1952, that 'She and her children shall be styled and known as the House and Family of Windsor, and that Her descendants, other than female descendants who marry, and their descendants, shall bear the name of Windsor.' In 1960 it was announced that future descendants would bear the surname Mountbatten-Windsor.

Following the death of King George V in 1936, the royal succession itself was straightforward within the House of Windsor, except for the abdication of King Edward VIII later in the same year.

The crisis soon passed, and the Duke of York succeeded as King George VI, ably supported by his wife, Queen Elizabeth, who was born Elizabeth Bowes Lyon and was the daughter of the Earl of Strathmore (see the Ancestry of HM Queen Elizabeth The Queen Mother, page 58).

King George VI reigned through the Second World War. He lived to see his daughter, Princess Elizabeth, married in 1947 to Prince Philip of Greece and Denmark, by then Lieutenant Philip Mountbatten, RN, and the birth of two grandchildren: Prince Charles and Princess Anne.

ABOVE: *King George VI*, Sir Gerald Kelly, 1938–45. This portrait, commissioned in 1938, kept Sir Gerald at work at Windsor Castle throughout the Second World War, and shows the King in his Coronation robes.

ABOVE RIGHT: *Elizabeth II*, Sir James Gunn, 1954–6. The Queen is depicted in her Coronation dress and robes. Many copies were made of this portrait to hang in British embassies throughout the world.

King George VI was succeeded by the present Sovereign, Queen Elizabeth II, who celebrated the Golden Jubilee of her reign in 2002. Her husband, Prince Philip, created Duke of Edinburgh at the time of their marriage, is also a descendant of Queen Victoria (see the Ancestry of HRH The Duke of Edinburgh, page 56).

Following Queen Elizabeth II, the line of succession is secure. Her son Charles, Prince of Wales, married in 1981; his first wife, Diana, Princess of Wales, was herself a descendant of the Stuart kings (see the Family Tree of Diana, Princess of Wales, page 60). They had two sons, Prince William and Prince Henry.

The family of King George V (detail), Sir John Lavery, 1923. King George V, as Admiral of the Fleet, with Queen Mary, The Prince of Wales (later The Duke of Windsor), and Princess Mary (The Princess Royal), in the White Drawing Room, Buckingham Palace.

House of Windsor

GEORGE V
(1865–1936)
KING OF THE UNITED KINGDOM OF GREAT BRITAIN AND NORTHERN IRELAND, EMPEROR OF INDIA
r.6 May 1910 – 20 January 1936

= 1893

Princess Victoria Mary of Teck
(1867–1953)
QUEEN MARY
(see FAMILY OF KING GEORGE III)

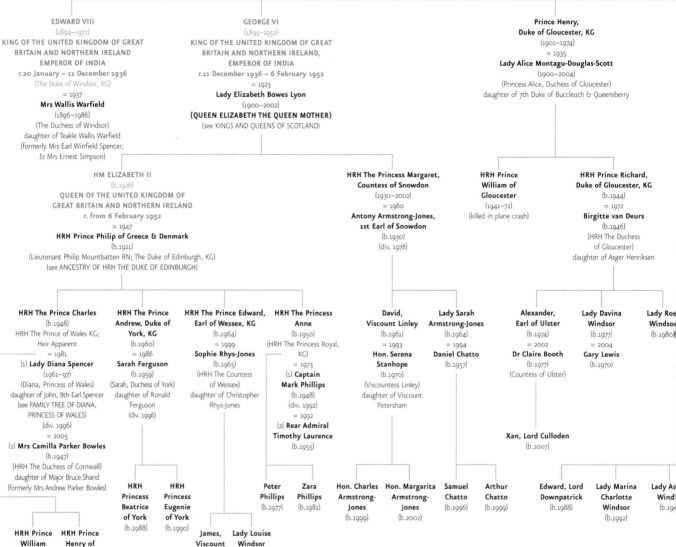

EDWARD VIII
(1894–1972)
KING OF THE UNITED KINGDOM OF GREAT BRITAIN AND NORTHERN IRELAND
EMPEROR OF INDIA
r.20 January – 11 December 1936
(The Duke of Windsor, KG)
= 1937
Mrs Wallis Warfield
(1896–1986)
(The Duchess of Windsor)
daughter of Teakle Wallis Warfield
(formerly Mrs Earl Winfield Spencer, & Mrs Ernest Simpson)

GEORGE VI
(1895–1952)
KING OF THE UNITED KINGDOM OF GREAT BRITAIN AND NORTHERN IRELAND,
EMPEROR OF INDIA
r.11 December 1936 – 6 February 1952
= 1923
Lady Elizabeth Bowes Lyon
(1900–2002)
(QUEEN ELIZABETH THE QUEEN MOTHER)
(see KINGS AND QUEENS OF SCOTLAND)

Prince Henry, Duke of Gloucester, KG
(1901–1974)
= 1935
Lady Alice Montagu-Douglas-Scott
(1900–2004)
(Princess Alice, Duchess of Gloucester)
daughter of 7th Duke of Buccleuch & Queensberry

HM ELIZABETH II
(b.1926)
QUEEN OF THE UNITED KINGDOM OF GREAT BRITAIN AND NORTHERN IRELAND
r. from 6 February 1952
= 1947
HRH Prince Philip of Greece & Denmark
(b.1921)
(Lieutenant Philip Mountbatten RN; The Duke of Edinburgh, KG)
(see ANCESTRY OF HRH THE DUKE OF EDINBURGH)

HRH The Princess Margaret, Countess of Snowdon
(1930–2002)
= 1960
Antony Armstrong-Jones, 1st Earl of Snowdon
(b.1930)
(div. 1978)

HRH Prince William of Gloucester
(1941–72)
(killed in plane crash)

HRH Prince Richard, Duke of Gloucester, KG
(b.1944)
= 1972
Birgitte van Deurs
(b.1946)
(HRH The Duchess of Gloucester)
daughter of Asger Henriksen

HRH The Prince Charles
(b.1948)
HRH The Prince of Wales KG;
Heir Apparent
= 1981
(1) **Lady Diana Spencer**
(1961–97)
(Diana, Princess of Wales)
daughter of John, 8th Earl Spencer
(see FAMILY TREE OF DIANA, PRINCESS OF WALES)
(div. 1996)
= 2005
(2) **Mrs Camilla Parker Bowles**
(b.1947)
(HRH The Duchess of Cornwall)
daughter of Major Bruce Shand
(formerly Mrs Andrew Parker Bowles)

HRH Prince William of Wales
(b.1982)

HRH Prince Henry of Wales
(b.1984)

HRH The Prince Andrew, Duke of York, KG
(b.1960)
= 1986
Sarah Ferguson
(b.1959)
(Sarah, Duchess of York)
daughter of Ronald Ferguson
(div. 1996)

HRH Princess Beatrice of York
(b.1988)

HRH Princess Eugenie of York
(b.1990)

HRH The Prince Edward, Earl of Wessex, KG
(b.1964)
= 1999
Sophie Rhys-Jones
(b.1965)
(HRH The Countess of Wessex)
daughter of Christopher Rhys-Jones

James, Viscount Severn
(b.2007)

Lady Louise Windsor
(b.2003)

HRH The Princess Anne
(b.1950)
(HRH The Princess Royal, KG)
= 1973
(1) **Captain Mark Phillips**
(b.1948)
(div. 1992)
= 1992
(2) **Rear Admiral Timothy Laurence**
(b.1955)

Peter Phillips
(b.1977)

Zara Phillips
(b.1981)

David, Viscount Linley
(b.1961)
= 1993
Hon. Serena Stanhope
(b.1970)
(Viscountess Linley)
daughter of Viscount Petersham

Hon. Charles Armstrong-Jones
(b.1999)

Hon. Margarita Armstrong-Jones
(b.2002)

Lady Sarah Armstrong-Jones
(b.1964)
= 1994
Daniel Chatto
(b.1957)

Samuel Chatto
(b.1996)

Arthur Chatto
(b.1999)

Alexander, Earl of Ulster
(b.1974)
= 2002
Dr Claire Booth
(b.1977)
(Countess of Ulster)

Xan, Lord Culloden
(b.2007)

Lady Davina Windsor
(b.1977)
= 2004
Gary Lewis
(b.1970)

Lady Ros
Windso
(b.1980)

Edward, Lord Downpatrick
(b.1988)

Lady Marina Charlotte Windsor
(b.1992)

Lady Ar
Wind
(b.19

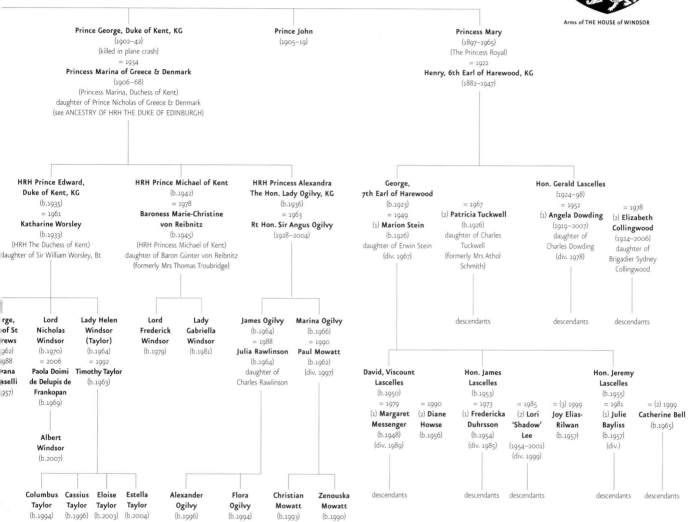

Arms of THE HOUSE of WINDSOR

Prince George, Duke of Kent, KG
(1902–42)
(killed in plane crash)
= 1934
Princess Marina of Greece & Denmark
(1906–68)
(Princess Marina, Duchess of Kent)
daughter of Prince Nicholas of Greece & Denmark
(see ANCESTRY OF HRH THE DUKE OF EDINBURGH)

Prince John
(1905–19)

Princess Mary
(1897–1965)
(The Princess Royal)
= 1922
Henry, 6th Earl of Harewood, KG
(1882–1947)

HRH Prince Edward, Duke of Kent, KG
(b.1935)
= 1961
Katharine Worsley
(b.1933)
(HRH The Duchess of Kent)
daughter of Sir William Worsley, Bt

HRH Prince Michael of Kent
(b.1942)
= 1978
Baroness Marie-Christine von Reibnitz
(b.1945)
(HRH Princess Michael of Kent)
daughter of Baron Günter von Reibnitz
(formerly Mrs Thomas Troubridge)

HRH Princess Alexandra The Hon. Lady Ogilvy, KG
(b.1936)
= 1963
Rt Hon. Sir Angus Ogilvy
(1928–2004)

George, 7th Earl of Harewood
(b.1923)
= 1949
(1) **Marion Stein**
(b.1926)
daughter of Erwin Stein
(div. 1967)

= 1967
(2) **Patricia Tuckwell**
(b.1926)
daughter of Charles Tuckwell
(formerly Mrs Athol Schmith)
descendants

Hon. Gerald Lascelles
(1924–98)
= 1952
(1) **Angela Dowding**
(1919–2007)
daughter of Charles Dowding
(div. 1978)
descendants

= 1978
(2) **Elizabeth Collingwood**
(1924–2006)
daughter of Brigadier Sydney Collingwood
descendants

rge,
of St
rews
962)
988
ana
selli
957)

Lord Nicholas Windsor
(b.1970)
= 2006
Paola Doimi de Delupis de Frankopan
(b.1969)

Albert Windsor
(b.2007)

Lady Helen Windsor (Taylor)
(b.1964)
= 1992
Timothy Taylor
(b.1963)

Columbus Taylor (b.1994)
Cassius Taylor (b.1996)
Eloise Taylor (b.2003)
Estella Taylor (b.2004)

Lord Frederick Windsor
(b.1979)

Lady Gabriella Windsor
(b.1981)

James Ogilvy
(b.1964)
= 1988
Julia Rawlinson
(b.1964)
daughter of Charles Rawlinson

Alexander Ogilvy (b.1996)
Flora Ogilvy (b.1994)

Marina Ogilvy
(b.1966)
= 1990
Paul Mowatt
(b.1962)
(div. 1997)

Christian Mowatt (b.1993)
Zenouska Mowatt (b.1990)

David, Viscount Lascelles
(b.1950)
= 1979
(1) **Margaret Messenger**
(b.1948)
(div. 1989)
descendants

= 1990
(2) **Diane Howse**
(b.1956)

Hon. James Lascelles
(b.1953)
= 1973
(1) **Fredericka Duhrsson**
(b.1954)
(div. 1985)
descendants

= 1985
(2) **Lori 'Shadow' Lee**
(1954–2001)
(div. 1999)
descendants

= (3) 1999
Joy Elias-Rilwan
(b.1957)

Hon. Jeremy Lascelles
(b.1955)
= 1981
(1) **Julie Bayliss**
(b.1957)
(div.)
descendants

= (2) 1999
Catherine Bell
(b.1965)
descendants

Four queens during the Golden Jubilee celebrations in 2002. On the left Queen Beatrix of The Netherlands, in the centre, Her Majesty The Queen, and on the right Queen Margrethe of Denmark. Behind Queen Margrethe is Queen Sofia of Spain.

Kings and Queens of Scotland

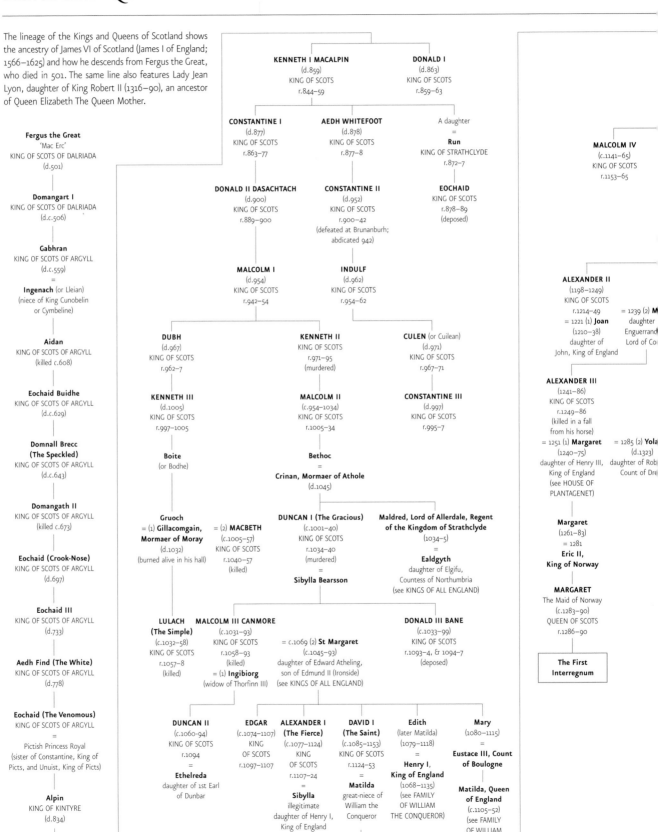

The lineage of the Kings and Queens of Scotland shows the ancestry of James VI of Scotland (James I of England; 1566–1625) and how he descends from Fergus the Great, who died in 501. The same line also features Lady Jean Lyon, daughter of King Robert II (1316–90), an ancestor of Queen Elizabeth The Queen Mother.

Fergus the Great
'Mac Erc'
KING OF SCOTS OF DALRIADA
(d.501)

Domangart I
KING OF SCOTS OF DALRIADA
(d.c.506)

Gabhran
KING OF SCOTS OF ARGYLL
(d.c.559)
=
Ingenach (or Lleian)
(niece of King Cunobelin or Cymbeline)

Aidan
KING OF SCOTS OF ARGYLL
(killed c.608)

Eochaid Buidhe
KING OF SCOTS OF ARGYLL
(d.c.629)

Domnall Brecc (The Speckled)
KING OF SCOTS OF ARGYLL
(d.c.643)

Domangath II
KING OF SCOTS OF ARGYLL
(killed c.673)

Eochaid (Crook-Nose)
KING OF SCOTS OF ARGYLL
(d.697)

Eochaid III
KING OF SCOTS OF ARGYLL
(d.733)

Aedh Find (The White)
KING OF SCOTS OF ARGYLL
(d.778)

Eochaid (The Venomous)
KING OF SCOTS OF ARGYLL
=
Pictish Princess Royal
(sister of Constantine, King of Picts, and Unuist, King of Picts)

Alpin
KING OF KINTYRE
(d.834)

KENNETH I MACALPIN
(d.859)
KING OF SCOTS
r.844–59

DONALD I
(d.863)
KING OF SCOTS
r.859–63

CONSTANTINE I
(d.877)
KING OF SCOTS
r.863–77

AEDH WHITEFOOT
(d.878)
KING OF SCOTS
r.877–8

A daughter
=
Run
KING OF STRATHCLYDE
r.872–7

DONALD II DASACHTACH
(d.900)
KING OF SCOTS
r.889–900

CONSTANTINE II
(d.952)
KING OF SCOTS
r.900–42
(defeated at Brunanburh; abdicated 942)

EOCHAID
KING OF SCOTS
r.878–89
(deposed)

MALCOLM I
(d.954)
KING OF SCOTS
r.942–54

INDULF
(d.962)
KING OF SCOTS
r.954–62

DUBH
(d.967)
KING OF SCOTS
r.962–7

KENNETH II
KING OF SCOTS
r.971–95
(murdered)

CULEN (or Cuilean)
(d.971)
KING OF SCOTS
r.967–71

KENNETH III
(d.1005)
KING OF SCOTS
r.997–1005

MALCOLM II
(c.954–1034)
KING OF SCOTS
r.1005–34

CONSTANTINE III
(d.997)
KING OF SCOTS
r.995–7

Boite
(or Bodhe)

Bethoc
=
Crinan, Mormaer of Athole
(d.1045)

Gruoch
= (1) **Gillacomgain, Mormaer of Moray**
(d.1032)
(burned alive in his hall)

= (2) **MACBETH**
(c.1005–57)
KING OF SCOTS
r.1040–57
(killed)

DUNCAN I (The Gracious)
(c.1001–40)
KING OF SCOTS
r.1034–40
(murdered)
=
Sibylla Bearsson

Maldred, Lord of Allerdale, Regent of the Kingdom of Strathclyde
(1034–5)
=
Ealdgyth
daughter of Elgifu, Countess of Northumbria
(see KINGS OF ALL ENGLAND)

LULACH (The Simple)
(c.1032–58)
KING OF SCOTS
r.1057–8
(killed)

MALCOLM III CANMORE
(c.1031–93)
KING OF SCOTS
r.1058–93
(killed)
= (1) **Ingibiorg**
(widow of Thorfinn III)

= c.1069 (2) **St Margaret**
(c.1045–93)
daughter of Edward Atheling, son of Edmund II (Ironside)
(see KINGS OF ALL ENGLAND)

DONALD III BANE
(c.1033–99)
KING OF SCOTS
r.1093–4, & 1094–7
(deposed)

DUNCAN II
(c.1060–94)
KING OF SCOTS
r.1094
=
Ethelreda
daughter of 1st Earl of Dunbar

EDGAR
(c.1074–1107)
KING OF SCOTS
r.1097–1107

ALEXANDER I (The Fierce)
(c.1077–1124)
KING OF SCOTS
r.1107–24
=
Sibylla
illegitimate daughter of Henry I, King of England

DAVID I (The Saint)
(c.1085–1153)
KING OF SCOTS
r.1124–53
=
Matilda
great-niece of William the Conqueror

Edith
(later Matilda)
(1079–1118)
=
Henry I, King of England
(1068–1135)
(see FAMILY OF WILLIAM THE CONQUEROR)

Mary
(1080–1115)
=
Eustace III, Count of Boulogne

Matilda, Queen of England
(c.1105–52)
(see FAMILY OF WILLIAM THE CONQUEROR)

MALCOLM IV
(c.1141–65)
KING OF SCOTS
r.1153–65

ALEXANDER II
(1198–1249)
KING OF SCOTS
r.1214–49
= 1221 (1) **Joan**
(1210–38)
daughter of John, King of England

= 1239 (2) **M**
daughter
Enguerrand
Lord of Co

ALEXANDER III
(1241–86)
KING OF SCOTS
r.1249–86
(killed in a fall from his horse)
= 1251 (1) **Margaret**
(1240–75)
daughter of Henry III, King of England
(see HOUSE OF PLANTAGENET)

= 1285 (2) **Yola**
(d.1323)
daughter of Rob
Count of Dre

Margaret
(1261–83)
= 1281
Eric II, King of Norway

MARGARET
The Maid of Norway
(c.1283–90)
QUEEN OF SCOTS
r.1286–90

The First Interregnum

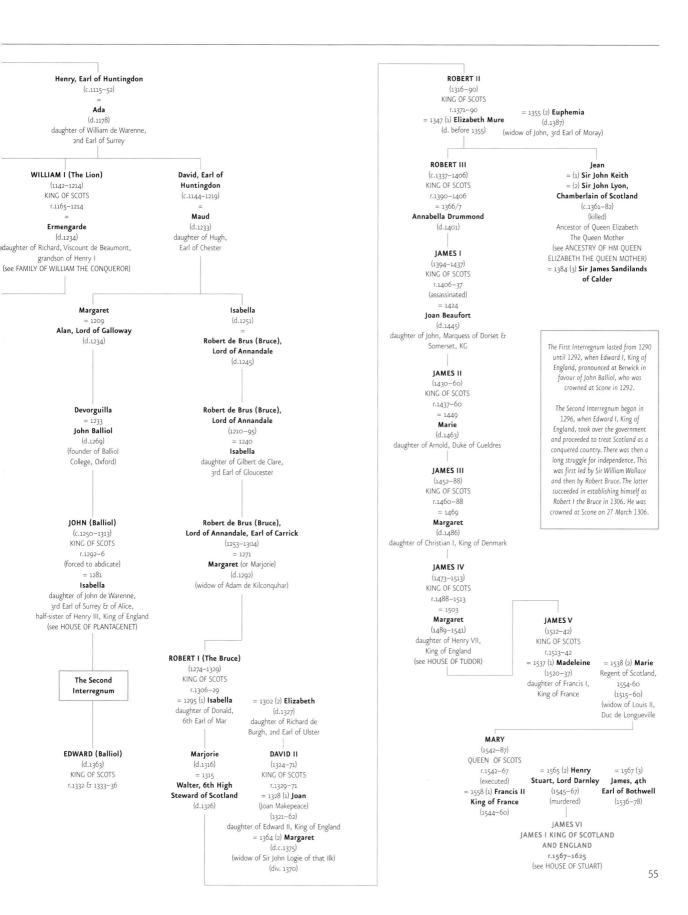

Henry, Earl of Huntingdon
(c.1115–52)
=
Ada
(d.1178)
daughter of William de Warenne,
2nd Earl of Surrey

WILLIAM I (The Lion)
(1142–1214)
KING OF SCOTS
r.1165–1214
=
Ermengarde
(d.1234)
daughter of Richard, Viscount de Beaumont,
grandson of Henry I
(see FAMILY OF WILLIAM THE CONQUEROR)

David, Earl of Huntingdon
(c.1144–1219)
=
Maud
(d.1233)
daughter of Hugh,
Earl of Chester

Margaret
= 1209
Alan, Lord of Galloway
(d.1234)

Devorguilla
= 1233
John Balliol
(d.1269)
(founder of Balliol
College, Oxford)

JOHN (Balliol)
(c.1250–1313)
KING OF SCOTS
r.1292–6
(forced to abdicate)
= 1281
Isabella
daughter of John de Warenne,
3rd Earl of Surrey & of Alice,
half-sister of Henry III, King of England
(see HOUSE OF PLANTAGENET)

The Second Interregnum

EDWARD (Balliol)
(d.1363)
KING OF SCOTS
r.1332 & 1333–36

Isabella
(d.1251)
=
Robert de Brus (Bruce), Lord of Annandale
(d.1245)

Robert de Brus (Bruce), Lord of Annandale
(1210–95)
= 1240
Isabella
daughter of Gilbert de Clare,
3rd Earl of Gloucester

Robert de Brus (Bruce), Lord of Annandale, Earl of Carrick
(1253–1304)
= 1271
Margaret (or Marjorie)
(d.1292)
(widow of Adam de Kilconquhar)

ROBERT I (The Bruce)
(1274–1329)
KING OF SCOTS
r.1306–29
= 1295 (1) **Isabella**
daughter of Donald,
6th Earl of Mar
= 1302 (2) **Elizabeth**
(d.1327)
daughter of Richard de
Burgh, 2nd Earl of Ulster

Marjorie
(d.1316)
= 1315
Walter, 6th High Steward of Scotland
(d.1326)

DAVID II
(1324–71)
KING OF SCOTS
r.1329–71
= 1328 (1) **Joan**
(Joan Makepeace)
(1321–62)
daughter of Edward II, King of England
= 1364 (2) **Margaret**
(d.c.1375)
(widow of Sir John Logie of that Ilk)
(div. 1370)

ROBERT II
(1316–90)
KING OF SCOTS
r.1371–90
= 1347 (1) **Elizabeth Mure**
(d. before 1355)
= 1355 (2) **Euphemia**
(d.1387)
(widow of John, 3rd Earl of Moray)

ROBERT III
(c.1337–1406)
KING OF SCOTS
r.1390–1406
= 1366/7
Annabella Drummond
(d.1401)

Jean
= (1) **Sir John Keith**
= (2) **Sir John Lyon, Chamberlain of Scotland**
(c.1361–82)
(killed)
Ancestor of Queen Elizabeth
The Queen Mother
(see ANCESTRY OF HM QUEEN
ELIZABETH THE QUEEN MOTHER)
= 1384 (3) **Sir James Sandilands of Calder**

JAMES I
(1394–1437)
KING OF SCOTS
r.1406–37
(assassinated)
= 1424
Joan Beaufort
(d.1445)
daughter of John, Marquess of Dorset &
Somerset, KG

JAMES II
(1430–60)
KING OF SCOTS
r.1437–60
= 1449
Marie
(d.1463)
daughter of Arnold, Duke of Gueldres

JAMES III
(1452–88)
KING OF SCOTS
r.1460–88
= 1469
Margaret
(d.1486)
daughter of Christian I, King of Denmark

JAMES IV
(1473–1513)
KING OF SCOTS
r.1488–1513
= 1503
Margaret
(1489–1541)
daughter of Henry VII,
King of England
(see HOUSE OF TUDOR)

The First Interregnum lasted from 1290 until 1292, when Edward I, King of England, pronounced at Berwick in favour of John Balliol, who was crowned at Scone in 1292.

The Second Interregnum began in 1296, when Edward I, King of England, took over the government and proceeded to treat Scotland as a conquered country. There was then a long struggle for independence. This was first led by Sir William Wallace and then by Robert Bruce. The latter succeeded in establishing himself as Robert I the Bruce in 1306. He was crowned at Scone on 27 March 1306.

JAMES V
(1512–42)
KING OF SCOTS
r.1513–42
= 1537 (1) **Madeleine**
(1520–37)
daughter of Francis I,
King of France
= 1538 (2) **Marie**
Regent of Scotland,
1554-60
(1515–60)
(widow of Louis II,
Duc de Longueville

MARY
(1542–87)
QUEEN OF SCOTS
r.1542–67
(executed)
= 1558 (1) **Francis II King of France**
(1544–60)
= 1565 (2) **Henry Stuart, Lord Darnley**
(1545–67)
(murdered)
= 1567 (3) **James, 4th Earl of Bothwell**
(1536–78)

JAMES VI
JAMES I KING OF SCOTLAND AND ENGLAND
r.1567–1625
(see HOUSE OF STUART)

ANCESTRY OF HRH THE DUKE OF EDINBURGH

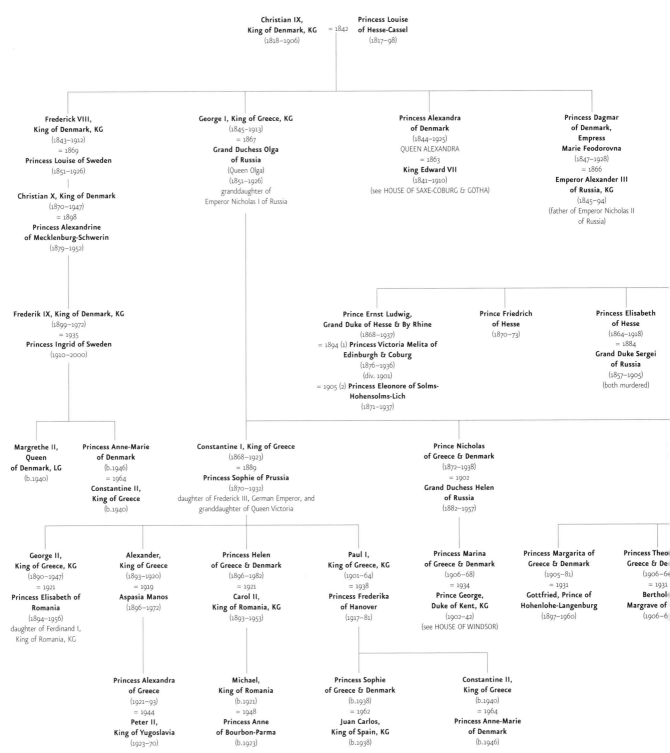

Christian IX, King of Denmark, KG (1818–1906) = 1842 **Princess Louise of Hesse-Cassel** (1817–98)

Frederick VIII, King of Denmark, KG
(1843–1912)
= 1869
Princess Louise of Sweden
(1851–1926)

Christian X, King of Denmark
(1870–1947)
= 1898
Princess Alexandrine of Mecklenburg-Schwerin
(1879–1952)

Frederik IX, King of Denmark, KG
(1899–1972)
= 1935
Princess Ingrid of Sweden
(1910–2000)

Margrethe II, Queen of Denmark, LG
(b.1940)

Princess Anne-Marie of Denmark
(b.1946)
= 1964
Constantine II, King of Greece
(b.1940)

George I, King of Greece, KG
(1845–1913)
= 1867
Grand Duchess Olga of Russia
(Queen Olga)
(1851–1926)
granddaughter of Emperor Nicholas I of Russia

Princess Alexandra of Denmark
(1844–1925)
QUEEN ALEXANDRA
= 1863
King Edward VII
(1841–1910)
(see HOUSE OF SAXE-COBURG & GOTHA)

Princess Dagmar of Denmark, Empress Marie Feodorovna
(1847–1928)
= 1866
Emperor Alexander III of Russia, KG
(1845–94)
(father of Emperor Nicholas II of Russia)

Prince Ernst Ludwig, Grand Duke of Hesse & By Rhine
(1868–1937)
= 1894 (1) **Princess Victoria Melita of Edinburgh & Coburg**
(1876–1936)
(div. 1901)
= 1905 (2) **Princess Eleonore of Solms-Hohensolms-Lich**
(1871–1937)

Prince Friedrich of Hesse
(1870–73)

Princess Elisabeth of Hesse
(1864–1918)
= 1884
Grand Duke Sergei of Russia
(1857–1905)
(both murdered)

Constantine I, King of Greece
(1868–1923)
= 1889
Princess Sophie of Prussia
(1870–1932)
daughter of Frederick III, German Emperor, and granddaughter of Queen Victoria

Prince Nicholas of Greece & Denmark
(1872–1938)
= 1902
Grand Duchess Helen of Russia
(1882–1957)

George II, King of Greece, KG
(1890–1947)
= 1921
Princess Elisabeth of Romania
(1894–1956)
daughter of Ferdinand I, King of Romania, KG

Alexander, King of Greece
(1893–1920)
= 1919
Aspasia Manos
(1896–1972)

Princess Helen of Greece & Denmark
(1896–1982)
= 1921
Carol II, King of Romania, KG
(1893–1953)

Paul I, King of Greece, KG
(1901–64)
= 1938
Princess Frederika of Hanover
(1917–81)

Princess Marina of Greece & Denmark
(1906–68)
= 1934
Prince George, Duke of Kent, KG
(1902–42)
(see HOUSE OF WINDSOR)

Princess Margarita of Greece & Denmark
(1905–81)
= 1931
Gottfried, Prince of Hohenlohe-Langenburg
(1897–1960)

Princess Theo Greece & De
(1906–6
= 1931
Berthol Margrave of
(1906–6

Princess Alexandra of Greece
(1921–93)
= 1944
Peter II, King of Yugoslavia
(1923–70)

Michael, King of Romania
(b.1921)
= 1948
Princess Anne of Bourbon-Parma
(b.1923)

Princess Sophie of Greece & Denmark
(b.1938)
= 1962
Juan Carlos, King of Spain, KG
(b.1938)

Constantine II, King of Greece
(b.1940)
= 1964
Princess Anne-Marie of Denmark
(b.1946)

This family tree of the ancestry of HRH Prince Philip, Duke of Edinburgh, shows select members of the family. Both Queen Alexandra and The Duke of Edinburgh descend from King Christian IX of Denmark (1818–1906). One can also trace the descent of Prince Philip from the Houses of Hesse-Darmstadt and Battenberg, and thus through his great-grandmother, Alice, Grand Duchess of Hesse (1843–78), the daughter of Queen Victoria. A number of kings and queens of Europe are included on this tree to show how The Duke of Edinburgh is related to the Queen of Denmark, the King of Spain, King Michael of Romania and King Constantine II of Greece. It includes his uncle (by marriage), the late King Gustaf VI Adolf of Sweden (1882–1973), and his great-aunt, Princess Alix of Hesse, the last Empress of Russia (1872–1918).

Arms of PRINCE PHILIP, THE DUKE OF EDINBURGH

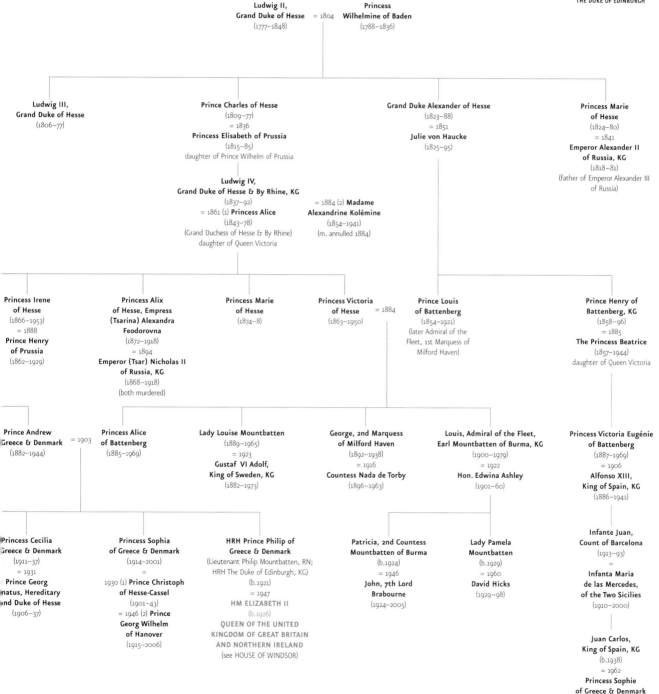

Ludwig II, Grand Duke of Hesse (1777–1848) = 1804 **Princess Wilhelmine of Baden** (1788–1836)

Ludwig III, Grand Duke of Hesse (1806–77)

Prince Charles of Hesse (1809–77) = 1836 **Princess Elisabeth of Prussia** (1815–85) daughter of Prince Wilhelm of Prussia

Grand Duke Alexander of Hesse (1823–88) = 1851 **Julie von Haucke** (1825–95)

Princess Marie of Hesse (1824–80) = 1841 **Emperor Alexander II of Russia, KG** (1818–81) (father of Emperor Alexander III of Russia)

Ludwig IV, Grand Duke of Hesse & By Rhine, KG (1837–92) = 1861 (1) **Princess Alice** (1843–78) (Grand Duchess of Hesse & By Rhine) daughter of Queen Victoria; = 1884 (2) **Madame Alexandrine Kolémine** (1854–1941) (m. annulled 1884)

Princess Irene of Hesse (1866–1953) = 1888 **Prince Henry of Prussia** (1862–1929)

Princess Alix of Hesse, Empress (Tsarina) Alexandra Feodorovna (1872–1918) = 1894 **Emperor (Tsar) Nicholas II of Russia, KG** (1868–1918) (both murdered)

Princess Marie of Hesse (1874–8)

Princess Victoria of Hesse (1863–1950) = 1884 **Prince Louis of Battenberg** (1854–1921) (later Admiral of the Fleet, 1st Marquess of Milford Haven)

Prince Henry of Battenberg, KG (1858–96) = 1885 **The Princess Beatrice** (1857–1944) daughter of Queen Victoria

Prince Andrew of Greece & Denmark (1882–1944) = 1903 **Princess Alice of Battenberg** (1885–1969)

Lady Louise Mountbatten (1889–1965) = 1923 **Gustaf VI Adolf, King of Sweden, KG** (1882–1973)

George, 2nd Marquess of Milford Haven (1892–1938) = 1916 **Countess Nada de Torby** (1896–1963)

Louis, Admiral of the Fleet, Earl Mountbatten of Burma, KG (1900–1979) = 1922 **Hon. Edwina Ashley** (1901–60)

Princess Victoria Eugénie of Battenberg (1887–1969) = 1906 **Alfonso XIII, King of Spain, KG** (1886–1941)

Princess Cecilia of Greece & Denmark (1911–37) = 1931 **Prince Georg Donatus, Hereditary Grand Duke of Hesse** (1906–37)

Princess Sophia of Greece & Denmark (1914–2001) = 1930 (1) **Prince Christoph of Hesse-Cassel** (1901–43) = 1946 (2) **Prince Georg Wilhelm of Hanover** (1915–2006)

HRH Prince Philip of Greece & Denmark (Lieutenant Philip Mountbatten, RN; HRH The Duke of Edinburgh, KG) (b.1921) = 1947 **HM ELIZABETH II** (b.1926) **QUEEN OF THE UNITED KINGDOM OF GREAT BRITAIN AND NORTHERN IRELAND** (see HOUSE OF WINDSOR)

Patricia, 2nd Countess Mountbatten of Burma (b.1924) = 1946 **John, 7th Lord Brabourne** (1924–2005)

Lady Pamela Mountbatten (b.1929) = 1960 **David Hicks** (1929–98)

Infante Juan, Count of Barcelona (1913–93) = **Infanta Maria de las Mercedes, of the Two Sicilies** (1910–2000)

Juan Carlos, King of Spain, KG (b.1938) = 1962 **Princess Sophie of Greece & Denmark** (b.1938)

Ancestry of Queen Elizabeth The Queen Mother

The tree mapping the ancestry of Queen Elizabeth The Queen Mother shows her descent through the Strathmore family from Lady Jean Lyon, the wife of Sir John Lyon and the daughter of Robert II, King of Scotland, and demonstrates her descent from Henry VII. In addition, the tree also features her Cavendish-Bentinck ancestors (from whom it was said sprang her longevity), the dukes of Portland and dukes of Devonshire; and the family of the great Duke of Wellington (1769–1852). It includes her cousin (and lady-in-waiting), Lady Victoria Wemyss (1890–1994), the last goddaughter of Queen Victoria to survive, who lived to be 104 years old.

Sir John Lyon
(c.1361–82)
=
Lady Jean Stewart
daughter of Robert II,
King of Scotland
(see KINGS AND QUEENS OF SCOTLAND)

Sir John Lyon
(c.1382–c.1435)
=
Elizabeth
daughter of Sir Patrick Graham & his wife, Euphemia, Countess Palatine of Strathearn

Patrick, 1st Lord Glamis
(c.1435–59)
=
Isabel
(c.1400–1484)
daughter of Sir Walter Ogilvy

John, 3rd Lord Glamis
(c.1459–97)
=
Elizabeth Scrymgeour

John, 4th Lord Glamis
(c.1477–1500)
=
Elizabeth
(c.1477–1526)
daughter of 2nd Lord Gray

John, 6th Lord Glamis
(c.1491–1528)
=
Jonet Douglas Master
(c.1512–37)

John, 7th Lord Glamis
(c.1528–59)
=
Janet Keith
daughter of William, 4th Earl Marischal

John, 8th Lord Glamis
(c.1544–1615)
=
Elizabeth Abernethy
(c.1543–81)
(widow of William Meldrum)

Patrick, 1st Earl of Kinghorne
(1575–1615)
= 1595
Anne
(1579–1618)
daughter of John, Earl of Tullibardine

John, 2nd Earl of Kinghorne
(1596–1646)
=
Lady Elizabeth Maule
(c.1624–59)

Patrick, 3rd Earl of Strathmore
(1643–95)
= 1662
Lady Helen Middleton
(c.1647–1708)

John, 4th Earl of Strathmore
(1663–1712)
= 1691
Lady Elizabeth Stanhope
(c.1663–1723)

Thomas, 8th Earl of Strathmore
(1704–53)
= 1736
Jean Nicholson
(1713–78)

John, 9th Earl of Strathmore
(1737–76)
= 1767
Mary Bowes
(1749–1800)

Thomas, 11th Earl of Strathmore
(1773–1846)
= 1800
Mary Carpenter
(1783–1811)

Henry, 1st Duke of Portland
(1682–1726)
= 1704
Lady Elizabeth Noel
(c.1688–1737)

William, 2nd Duke of Portland, KG
(1708–62)
Lady Margaret Harley
(1715–85)

Charles, 3rd Earl of Cork
(c.1674–1704)
= 1687/8
Juliana Noel
(1672–1750)

Richard, 4th Earl of Cork, KG
(1695–1753)
= 1720
Lady Dorothy Savile
(1699–1758)
daughter of William, Marquess of Ha

Charlotte Boyle, Baroness Clifford
(1731–54)
= 1748
William, 4th Duke of Devonshire, KG
(1720–64)

William, 3rd Duke of Portland, KG
(1738–1809)
= 1766
Lady Dorothy Cavendish
(1750–94)

Thomas, Lord Glamis
(1801–34)
= 1820
Charlotte Grimstead
(1797–1881)

Claude, 13th Earl of Strathmore
(1824–1904)
= 1853
Frances Smith
(1832–1922)

Rev. Charles Cavendish-Bentinck
(1817–65)
= 1859
Caroline Burnaby
(1833–89)

Claude, 14th Earl of Strathmore, KG
(1855–1944)
= 1881
Nina Cavendish-Bentinck
(1862–1938)

Lady Violet Bowes Lyon
(1882–93)

Lady Mary Bowes Lyon
(1883–1961)
= 1910
16th Baron Elphinstone
(1869–1955)

Patrick, 15th Earl of Strathmore
(1884–1949)
= 1908
Lady Dorothy Osborne
(1888–1946)

Hon. John Bowes Lyon
(1886–1930)
= 1914
Hon. Fenella Hepburn-Stuart
(1889–1966)

Hon. Alexander Bowes Lyon
(1887–1911)

Hon. Fergus Bowes Lyon
(1889–1915)
(killed in the First World War)
= 1914
Lady Christian Dawson-Damer
(1890–1959)

Lady Rose Bowes Lyon
(1890–1967)
= 1916
4th Earl Granville, KG
(1880–1953)

Hon. Michael Bowes Lyon
(1893–1953)
= 1928
Elizabeth Cator
(1899–1959)

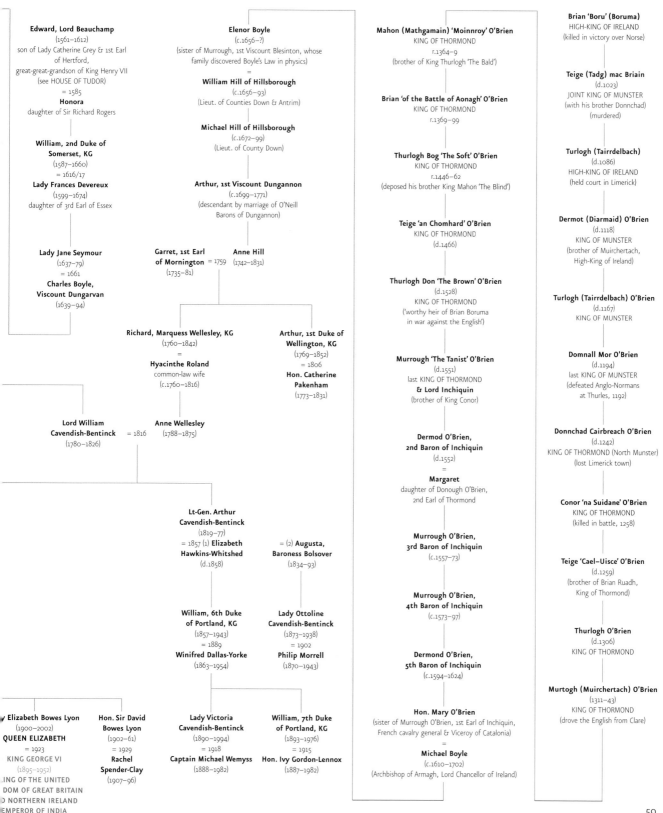

Edward, Lord Beauchamp
(1561–1612)
son of Lady Catherine Grey & 1st Earl of Hertford,
great-great-grandson of King Henry VII
(see HOUSE OF TUDOR)
= 1585
Honora
daughter of Sir Richard Rogers

William, 2nd Duke of Somerset, KG
(1587–1660)
= 1616/17
Lady Frances Devereux
(1599–1674)
daughter of 3rd Earl of Essex

Lady Jane Seymour
(1637–79)
= 1661
Charles Boyle, Viscount Dungarvan
(1639–94)

Elenor Boyle
(c.1656–?)
(sister of Murrough, 1st Viscount Blesinton, whose family discovered Boyle's Law in physics)
=
William Hill of Hillsborough
(c.1656–93)
(Lieut. of Counties Down & Antrim)

Michael Hill of Hillsborough
(c.1672–99)
(Lieut. of County Down)

Arthur, 1st Viscount Dungannon
(c.1699–1771)
(descendant by marriage of O'Neill Barons of Dungannon)

Garret, 1st Earl of Mornington (1735–81) = 1759 **Anne Hill** (1742–1831)

Richard, Marquess Wellesley, KG
(1760–1842)
=
Hyacinthe Roland
common-law wife
(c.1760–1816)

Arthur, 1st Duke of Wellington, KG
(1769–1852)
= 1806
Hon. Catherine Pakenham
(1773–1831)

Lord William Cavendish-Bentinck (1780–1826) = 1816 **Anne Wellesley** (1788–1875)

Lt-Gen. Arthur Cavendish-Bentinck
(1819–77)
= 1857 (1) **Elizabeth Hawkins-Whitshed**
(d.1858)
= (2) **Augusta, Baroness Bolsover**
(1834–93)

William, 6th Duke of Portland, KG
(1857–1943)
= 1889
Winifred Dallas-Yorke
(1863–1954)

Lady Ottoline Cavendish-Bentinck
(1873–1938)
= 1902
Philip Morrell
(1870–1943)

Elizabeth Bowes Lyon
(1900–2002)
QUEEN ELIZABETH
= 1923
KING GEORGE VI
(1895–1952)
ING OF THE UNITED
DOM OF GREAT BRITAIN
D NORTHERN IRELAND
EMPEROR OF INDIA

Hon. Sir David Bowes Lyon
(1902–61)
= 1929
Rachel Spender-Clay
(1907–96)

Lady Victoria Cavendish-Bentinck
(1890–1994)
= 1918
Captain Michael Wemyss
(1888–1982)

William, 7th Duke of Portland, KG
(1893–1976)
= 1915
Hon. Ivy Gordon-Lennox
(1887–1982)

Mahon (Mathgamain) 'Moinnroy' O'Brien
KING OF THORMOND
r.1364–9
(brother of King Thurlogh 'The Bald')

Brian 'of the Battle of Aonagh' O'Brien
KING OF THORMOND
r.1369–99

Thurlogh Bog 'The Soft' O'Brien
KING OF THORMOND
r.1446–62
(deposed his brother King Mahon 'The Blind')

Teige 'an Chomhard' O'Brien
KING OF THORMOND
(d.1466)

Thurlogh Don 'The Brown' O'Brien
(d.1528)
KING OF THORMOND
('worthy heir of Brian Boruma in war against the English')

Murrough 'The Tanist' O'Brien
(d.1551)
last KING OF THORMOND
& Lord Inchiquin
(brother of King Conor)

Dermod O'Brien, 2nd Baron of Inchiquin
(d.1552)
=
Margaret
daughter of Donough O'Brien, 2nd Earl of Thormond

Murrough O'Brien, 3rd Baron of Inchiquin
(c.1557–73)

Murrough O'Brien, 4th Baron of Inchiquin
(c.1573–97)

Dermond O'Brien, 5th Baron of Inchiquin
(c.1594–1624)

Hon. Mary O'Brien
(sister of Murrough O'Brien, 1st Earl of Inchiquin, French cavalry general & Viceroy of Catalonia)
=
Michael Boyle
(c.1610–1702)
(Archbishop of Armagh, Lord Chancellor of Ireland)

Brian 'Boru' (Boruma)
HIGH-KING OF IRELAND
(killed in victory over Norse)

Teige (Tadg) mac Briain
(d.1023)
JOINT KING OF MUNSTER
(with his brother Donnchad)
(murdered)

Turlogh (Tairrdelbach)
(d.1086)
HIGH-KING OF IRELAND
(held court in Limerick)

Dermot (Diarmaid) O'Brien
(d.1118)
KING OF MUNSTER
(brother of Muirchertach, High-King of Ireland)

Turlogh (Tairrdelbach) O'Brien
(d.1167)
KING OF MUNSTER

Domnall Mor O'Brien
(d.1194)
last KING OF MUNSTER
(defeated Anglo-Normans at Thurles, 1192)

Donnchad Cairbreach O'Brien
(d.1242)
KING OF THORMOND (North Munster)
(lost Limerick town)

Conor 'na Suidane' O'Brien
KING OF THORMOND
(killed in battle, 1258)

Teige 'Cael-Uisce' O'Brien
(d.1259)
(brother of Brian Ruadh, King of Thormond)

Thurlogh O'Brien
(d.1306)
KING OF THORMOND

Murtogh (Muirchertach) O'Brien
(1311–43)
KING OF THORMOND
(drove the English from Clare)

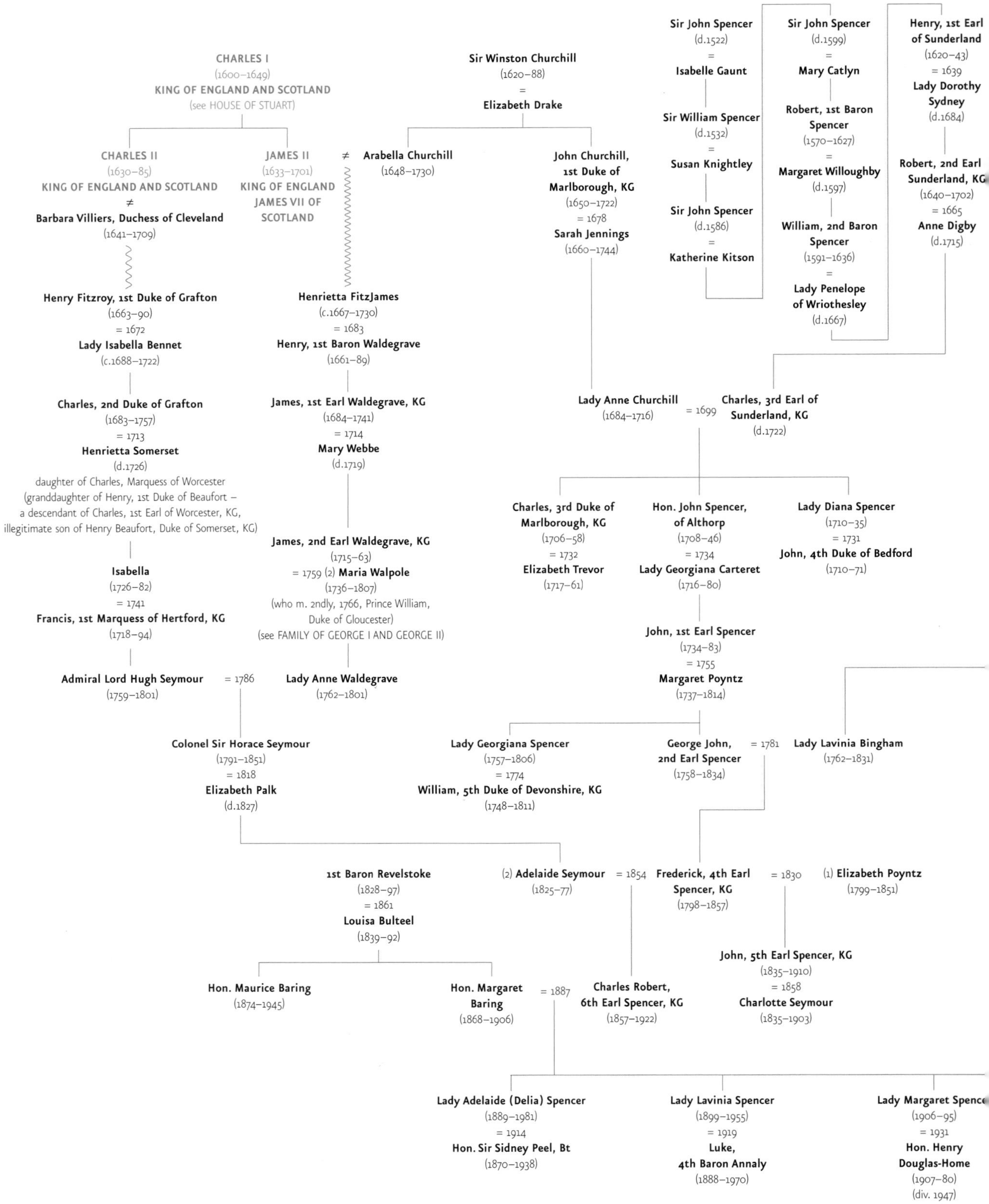

Family Tree of Diana, Princess of Wales

The family tree of Diana, Princess of Wales, charts her Spencer ancestors, and shows three lines of descent from Charles II (1630–85). She also descended from the 1st Duke of Marlborough (1650–1722) and was collaterally related to a number of notable people, including the writer Maurice Baring (1874–1945).

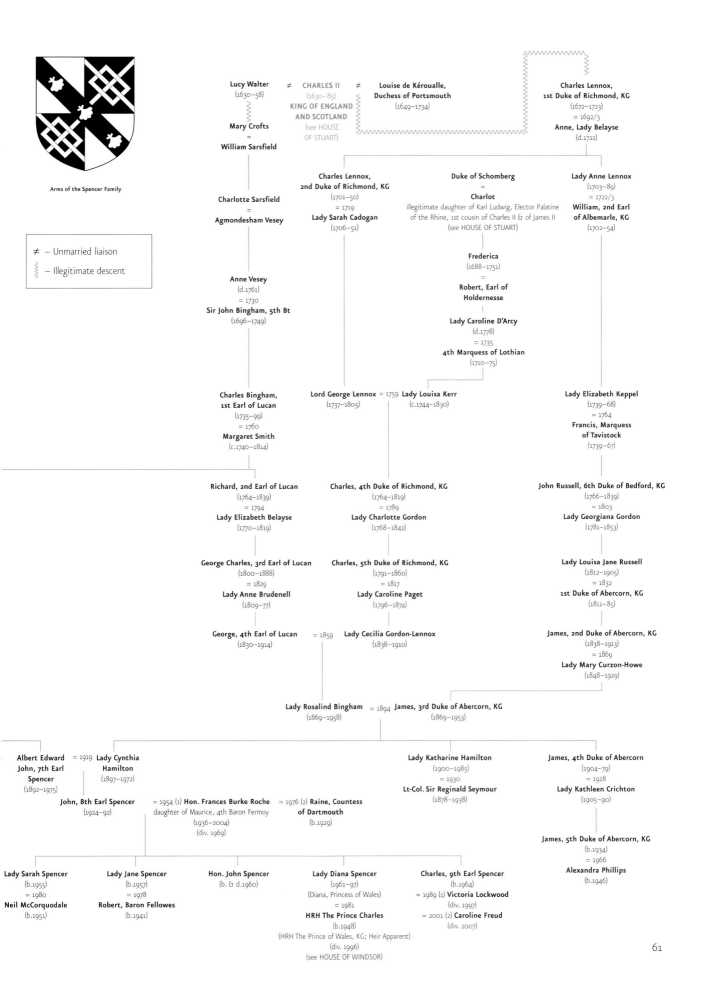

Arms of the Spencer Family

≠ – Unmarried liaison

(wavy line) – Illegitimate descent

Lucy Walter (1630–58) ≠ **CHARLES II** (1630–85) KING OF ENGLAND AND SCOTLAND (see HOUSE OF STUART) ≠ **Louise de Kéroualle, Duchess of Portsmouth** (1649–1734)

Mary Crofts
=
William Sarsfield

Charles Lennox, 1st Duke of Richmond, KG
(1672–1723)
= 1692/3
Anne, Lady Belayse
(d.1722)

Charlotte Sarsfield
=
Agmondesham Vesey

Charles Lennox, 2nd Duke of Richmond, KG
(1701–50)
= 1719
Lady Sarah Cadogan
(1706–51)

Duke of Schomberg
=
Charlot
illegitimate daughter of Karl Ludwig, Elector Palatine of the Rhine, 1st cousin of Charles II & of James II
(see HOUSE OF STUART)

Lady Anne Lennox
(1703–89)
= 1722/3
William, 2nd Earl of Albemarle, KG
(1702–54)

Frederica
(1688–1751)
=
Robert, Earl of Holdernesse

Anne Vesey
(d.1761)
= 1730
Sir John Bingham, 5th Bt
(1696–1749)

Lady Caroline D'Arcy
(d.1778)
= 1735
4th Marquess of Lothian
(1710–75)

Charles Bingham, 1st Earl of Lucan
(1735–99)
= 1760
Margaret Smith
(c.1740–1814)

Lord George Lennox (1737–1805) = 1759 **Lady Louisa Kerr** (c.1744–1830)

Lady Elizabeth Keppel
(1739–68)
= 1764
Francis, Marquess of Tavistock
(1739–67)

Richard, 2nd Earl of Lucan
(1764–1839)
= 1794
Lady Elizabeth Belayse
(1770–1819)

Charles, 4th Duke of Richmond, KG
(1764–1819)
= 1789
Lady Charlotte Gordon
(1768–1842)

John Russell, 6th Duke of Bedford, KG
(1766–1839)
= 1803
Lady Georgiana Gordon
(1781–1853)

George Charles, 3rd Earl of Lucan
(1800–1888)
= 1829
Lady Anne Brudenell
(1809–77)

Charles, 5th Duke of Richmond, KG
(1791–1860)
= 1817
Lady Caroline Paget
(1796–1874)

Lady Louisa Jane Russell
(1812–1905)
= 1832
1st Duke of Abercorn, KG
(1811–85)

George, 4th Earl of Lucan (1830–1914) = 1859 **Lady Cecilia Gordon-Lennox** (1838–1910)

James, 2nd Duke of Abercorn, KG
(1838–1913)
= 1869
Lady Mary Curzon-Howe
(1848–1929)

Lady Rosalind Bingham (1869–1958) = 1894 **James, 3rd Duke of Abercorn, KG** (1869–1953)

Albert Edward John, 7th Earl Spencer (1892–1975) = 1919 **Lady Cynthia Hamilton** (1897–1972)

Lady Katharine Hamilton
(1900–1985)
= 1930
Lt-Col. Sir Reginald Seymour
(1878–1938)

James, 4th Duke of Abercorn
(1904–79)
= 1928
Lady Kathleen Crichton
(1905–90)

John, 8th Earl Spencer (1924–92) = 1954 (1) **Hon. Frances Burke Roche** daughter of Maurice, 4th Baron Fermoy (1936–2004) (div. 1969) = 1976 (2) **Raine, Countess of Dartmouth** (b.1929)

James, 5th Duke of Abercorn, KG
(b.1934)
= 1966
Alexandra Phillips
(b.1946)

Lady Sarah Spencer
(b.1955)
= 1980
Neil McCorquodale
(b.1951)

Lady Jane Spencer
(b.1957)
= 1978
Robert, Baron Fellowes
(b.1941)

Hon. John Spencer
(b. & d.1960)

Lady Diana Spencer
(1961–97)
(Diana, Princess of Wales)
= 1981
HRH The Prince Charles
(b.1948)
(HRH The Prince of Wales, KG; Heir Apparent)
(div. 1996)
(see HOUSE OF WINDSOR)

Charles, 9th Earl Spencer
(b.1964)
= 1989 (1) **Victoria Lockwood**
(div. 1997)
= 2001 (2) **Caroline Freud**
(div. 2007)

Ancestry of
HRH Prince William of Wales

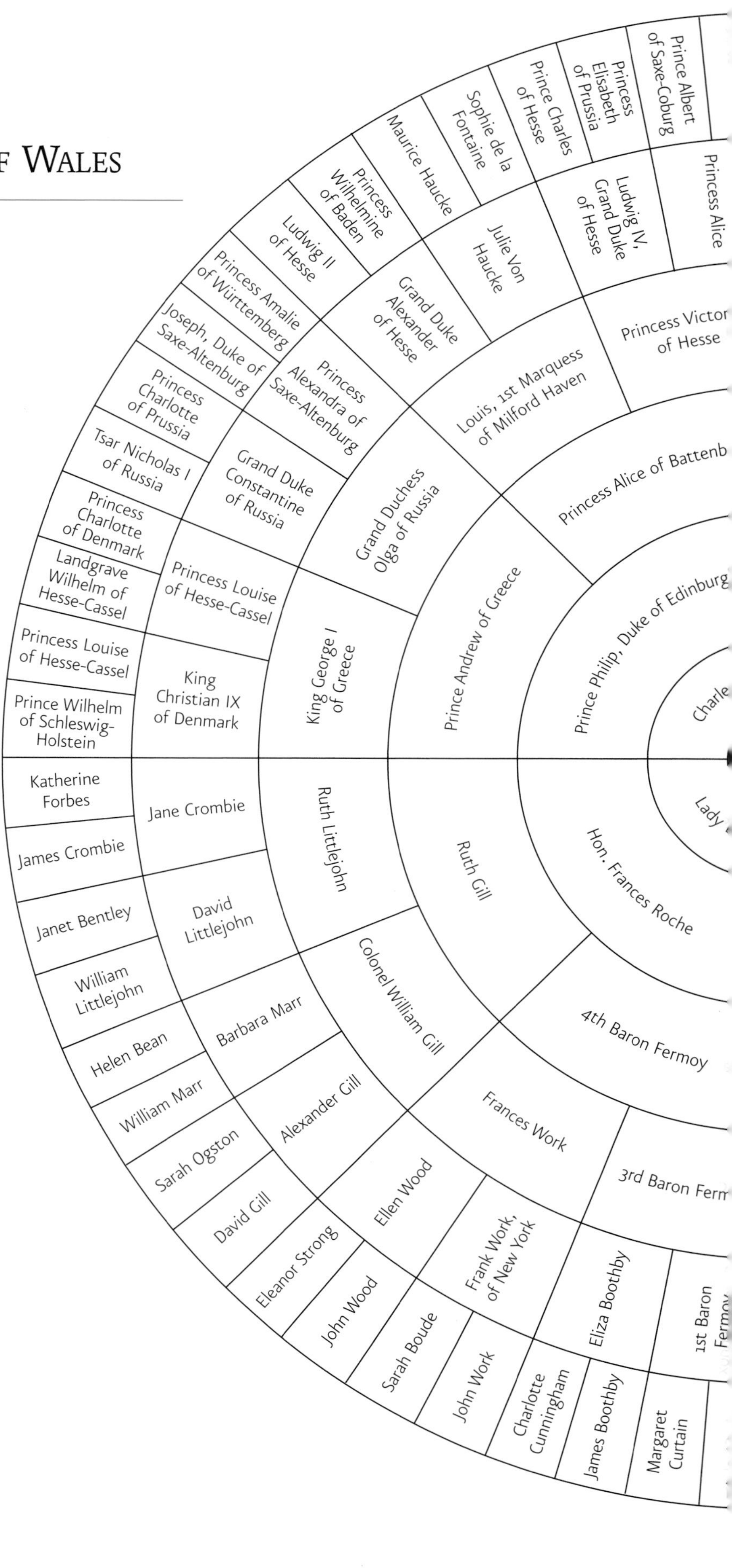

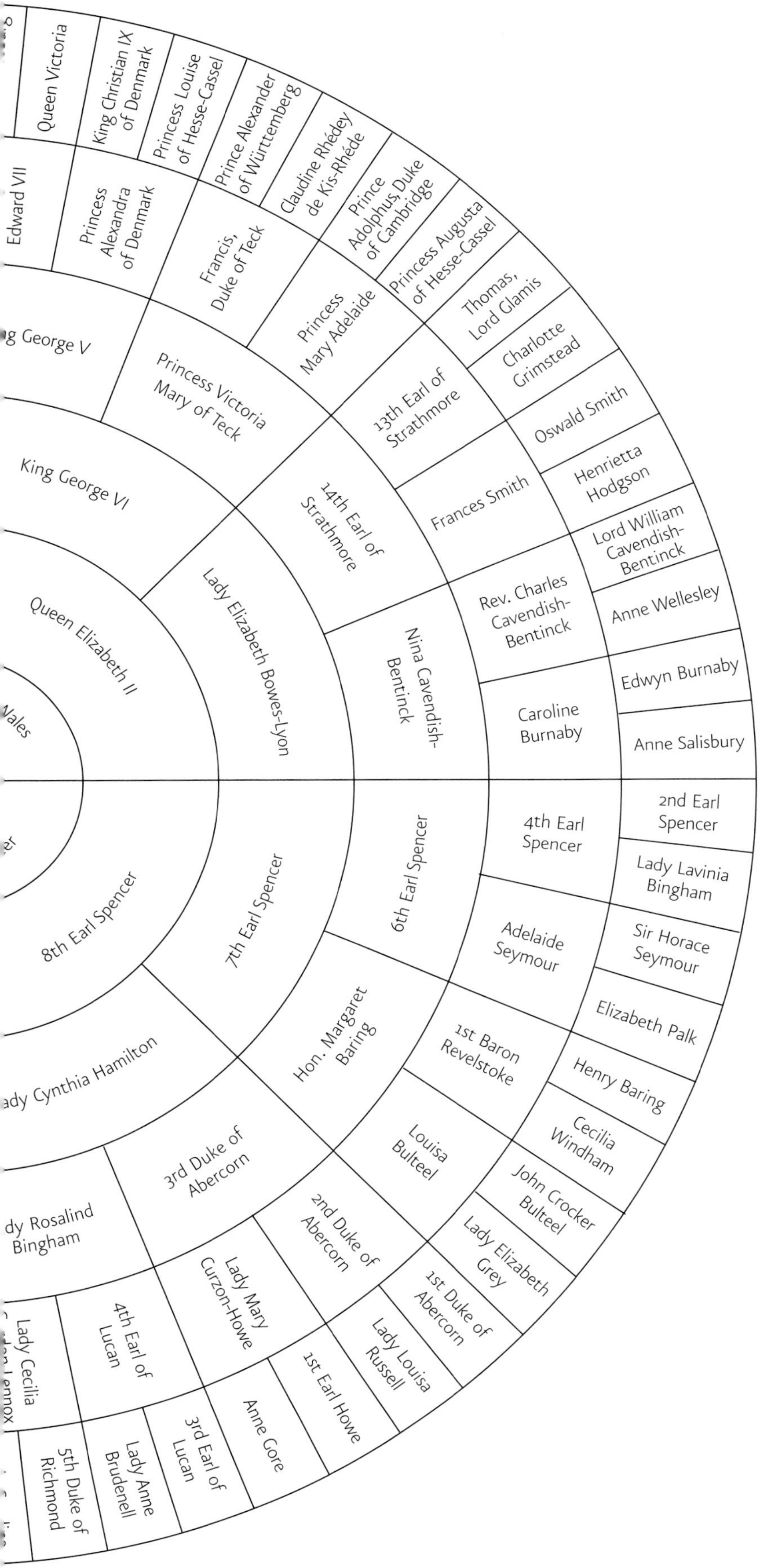

Queen Victoria
King Christian IX of Denmark
Princess Louise of Hesse-Cassel
Prince Alexander of Württemberg
Claudine Rhédey de Kis-Rhéde
Prince Adolphus, Duke of Cambridge
Princess Augusta of Hesse-Cassel
Thomas, Lord Glamis
Charlotte Grimstead
Oswald Smith
Henrietta Hodgson
Lord William Cavendish-Bentinck
Anne Wellesley
Edwyn Burnaby
Anne Salisbury
2nd Earl Spencer
Lady Lavinia Bingham
Sir Horace Seymour
Elizabeth Palk
Henry Baring
Cecilia Windham
John Crocker Bulteel
Lady Elizabeth Grey
1st Duke of Abercorn
Lady Louisa Russell
1st Earl Howe
Anne Gore
3rd Earl of Lucan
Lady Anne Brudenell
5th Duke of Richmond
Edward VII
Princess Alexandra of Denmark
Francis, Duke of Teck
Princess Mary Adelaide
13th Earl of Strathmore
Frances Smith
Rev. Charles Cavendish-Bentinck
Caroline Burnaby
4th Earl Spencer
Adelaide Seymour
1st Baron Revelstoke
Louisa Bulteel
2nd Duke of Abercorn
Lady Mary Curzon-Howe
4th Earl of Lucan
Lady Cecilia
g George V
Princess Victoria Mary of Teck
14th Earl of Strathmore
Nina Cavendish-Bentinck
6th Earl Spencer
Hon. Margaret Baring
3rd Duke of Abercorn
dy Rosalind Bingham
King George VI
Lady Elizabeth Bowes-Lyon
7th Earl Spencer
ady Cynthia Hamilton
Queen Elizabeth II
8th Earl Spencer

Supplementary Notes

THE BILL OF RIGHTS, 1689

The basis for the present rule of succession was determined in the constitutional struggles of the 17th century, culminating in the Bill of Rights which guaranteed the rights of Parliament against the Sovereign. In 1688 William, Prince of Orange, the Stadtholder of the Netherlands, was invited to come to England to battle against the reigning monarch, his father-in-law James II, in an effort to safeguard the Protestant interest. James II had determined on a course to bring England back to Catholicism, and now finding opposition on all sides, he threw the Great Seal of England into the Thames and fled abroad.

In 1689 a convention of Parliament drew up a declaration of rights which affirmed the rights and liberties of the people. The Bill of Rights received the royal assent on 16 December 1689. The Bill made the Sovereign subject to the laws of the land, and linked the succession to the acceptance by the new Sovereign of the rights of the people. It is this Bill that excluded James II (who was still alive) and any of his descendants from succeeding to the throne. The Bill also prevented any Roman Catholics – or those married to Catholics – from ascending the throne. The throne was therefore offered not to James II's infant son, but to his impeccably Protestant daughter Mary and her husband, William of Orange, who accepted the Bill of Rights.

The Sovereign was bound to agree in the Coronation Oath to govern 'according to the statutes of Parliament agreed upon and the laws and customs of the same'. The Bill ordained that parliaments were to be summoned frequently and it made the monarch dependent on Parliament for funds – and thus established the guidelines for a successful constitutional monarchy.

THE ACT OF SETTLEMENT, 1701

The Act of Settlement further limited the powers of the Crown and secured the rights and liberties of the people, and confirmed that it was for Parliament to determine the title to the throne. It followed in the wake of the Bill of Rights and its main purpose was to secure the Protestant succession. The Bill of Rights had provided that the crown would pass to the heirs of Mary II, then to Queen Anne and her heirs, but neither Queen left surviving issue. There was a need to identify the rightful heir to the throne. Sophia, Electress of Hanover, was selected to succeed, being the next eligible Protestant in line. A great number of Catholic candidates were passed over.

The Act confirmed further conditions: the Sovereign could not be a Roman Catholic or be married to one. He or she had to maintain the Church of England (and, following the Act of Union of 1707, the Church of Scotland). The Sovereign was to be in communion with the Church of England, and had to promise to maintain the Protestant religion. Parliamentary consent was required for the Sovereign to engage in war, and judges were made independent of 'the royal pleasure'. The Act marked another significant step towards the modern constitutional monarchy.

THE ROYAL MARRIAGES ACT, 1772

The Royal Marriages Act of 1772 was passed because George III was displeased that two of his brothers – William, Duke of Gloucester, and Henry, Duke of Cumberland – had married commoners, without his knowledge or consent. It granted the Sovereign some powers to prevent or delay unsuitable marriages into the family, which were not legal without his consent.

The purpose of the Act was to reserve to the monarch (and to his successors) the right to approve the marriages of any descendant of George II, other than the issue of princesses who married into foreign families. It stated: 'We have taken this weighty matter into our serious consideration; and being sensible that marriages in the royal family are of the highest importance to the state, and that therefore Kings of this realm have ever been entrusted with the care and approbation thereof.'

The Act decreed that the King's permission was required to be signified 'under the great seal, and declared in council'. Any marriage or matrimonial contract entered into without such consent would be 'null and void, to all intents and purposes whatsoever'. There is one interesting proviso. When a member of the royal family reached the age of twenty-five, he or she could give notice to the Privy Council of their intention to marry and, even if the Sovereign's permission were withheld, after a year they would be free to marry, unless within that year 'both houses of parliament... expressly declare their disapprobation of such intended marriage'.

The Royal Marriages Act is still in force today, and all descendants of George II (other than those who also descend from someone who married into a foreign royal house) are bound by it.

COUNSELLORS OF STATE

Counsellors of State are appointed to execute the functions of the Sovereign in the absence of the reigning King or Queen, especially when abroad. For example, when Henry V and William III were abroad fighting, and when George I was in Hanover, each appointed a Guardian of the Realm or *Custos Regni*.

King George V appointed Counsellors of State when he went to India in 1911–12, and when he was ill in 1928–9. Modern-day Counsellors of State are appointed by letters patent under the terms of the Regency Acts, of which there have been three, in 1937, 1943 and 1953. They are appointed for a limited period of time and for a specific reason.

Under the Regency Acts of 1937–53, the Counsellors are the spouse of the Sovereign and the next five in line to the throne who have reached the age of twenty-one (or eighteen if the heir apparent). (It was the next four in line while Queen Elizabeth The Queen Mother was alive, as she was made eligible for appointment and served frequently until the 1990s.) At present, the six Counsellors of State are The Duke of Edinburgh, The Prince of Wales, The Duke of York, The Earl of Wessex, The Princess Royal and Peter Phillips. Prince William and Prince Henry are eligible to be Counsellors of State.

Counsellors of State are empowered to hold Privy Councils and signify The Queen's approval in Council, to issue commissions for giving the royal assent to Acts of Parliament (with the exception of Acts that affect royal styles or the Act of Settlement), to approve and sign proclamations, warrants and other such documents, and to exercise the royal prerogative and other statutory powers enabling The Queen to act for the safety and good government of the United Kingdom and colonies.

Counsellors are specifically not allowed to dissolve Parliament (other than on the express command of the Sovereign), or to grant titles, ranks or dignities in the peerage. They are allowed to refuse to act if it appears to them that they should take specific instruction from the Sovereign. Usually two Counsellors act together.

In their time, members of the Royal Family such as Princess Margaret, Prince Henry, Duke of Gloucester, the late Princess Royal, and even Princess Arthur of Connaught and the Countess of Southesk (granddaughters of King Edward VII) all acted as Counsellors of State, as did the present Earl of Harewood when a young man, all owing to their position in line of succession to the throne.

ROYAL TITLES

Certain titles are traditionally associated with the royal family.

The Heir Apparent

In the peerage of England, the heir apparent is automatically **Duke of Cornwall** if the eldest son of the Sovereign, and in Scotland he is **Duke of Rothesay**, **Earl of Carrick**, **Baron of Renfrew**, **Lord of the Isles** and **Great Steward of Scotland**. Richard, second son of King John, was also Earl of Cornwall, but the title died out in 1300. Cornwall has been associated with the heir to the throne since Edward III created his son Edward **Duke of Cornwall** in 1337. The Scottish titles date back to 1398.

The title of **Earl of Chester** was conferred on Edward, eldest son of Henry III, in 1254. In 1301 Edward I conferred the title of **Prince of Wales** on his eldest surviving son, who became Edward II in 1307. Edward II gave his son (later Edward III) the earldom of Chester. Since the days of Edward III, the two titles have always been conferred together. In 1911, Edward, son of George V, was formally invested as Prince of Wales at Caernarvon Castle, as was Prince Charles in 1969.

Duke of York

The title of **Duke of York** has always been a royal one and has come to be bestowed on the second son of the Sovereign. It was first conferred on Edmund, fifth son of Edward III, by Richard II in 1385. The title has frequently reverted to the Crown as several dukes of York have become Prince of Wales or King. The title is currently held by Prince Andrew.

Duke of Gloucester

The title of **Duke of Gloucester** has always been a royal one. The first duke was Thomas of Woodstock, seventh son of Edward III, and perhaps the most famous holder of the title was the future Richard III. The title has sometimes died out but periodically been revived: in 1659 for the youngest son of Charles I; in 1689 for Queen Anne's sole surviving child; in 1764 for a brother of George III; and in 1928 for Prince Henry, third son of King George V. It is now held by his second and only surviving son, Prince Richard.

Duke of Kent

The title of **Earl of Kent** was conferred on Odo, Bishop of Bayeux, by his half-brother, William I, and has been re-created several times since. A dukedom of this name was held by the non-royal Henry Grey from 1710 to 1740. Queen Victoria's father held the title until his death in 1820. Queen Victoria gave it as an earldom to her second son, Prince Alfred, Duke of Edinburgh, and it became a dukedom once more when conferred on Prince George, fourth son of King George V. It is currently held by his elder son, Prince Edward.

Duke of Edinburgh

Frederick, eldest son of George, Prince of Wales (later George II), was the first **Duke of Edinburgh** in 1726. The dukedom merged with the Crown on the succession in 1760 of George III, who gave it as a second dukedom to the Duke of Gloucester in 1764. The title died out, to be revived by Queen Victoria for her second son, Prince Alfred, in 1866. After his death in 1900, the title again became extinct. King George VI conferred it on Lieutenant Philip Mountbatten, RN, when he married Princess Elizabeth in 1947.

Other Royal Dukedoms

There have been other royal dukedoms, all of which have become extinct. The dukedom of **Clarence** has always been royal and was conferred on George, brother of Edward IV; on the son of George III who became William IV; and on the eldest son of Albert Edward, Prince of Wales (later King Edward VII), Prince Albert Victor, who died in 1892. There have been dukes of **Albany**, of which the last holder was Charles Edward, a grandson of Queen Victoria. During the First World War he was struck from the roll of peers, as was the Duke of **Cumberland**, on account of German connections. The dukedom of **Cambridge** was revived as a marquessate for Queen Mary's brother, but died out in 1981; the dukedom of **Connaught**, held by Queen Victoria's third son, Prince Arthur, died out with his grandson in 1943.

There have also been dukes of **Kendal** and **Sussex**, and The Queen is **Duke of Lancaster** (not Duchess) to this day.

The Princess Royal

The title of **The Princess Royal** is reserved for the eldest daughter of the Sovereign, and is held for life. It is granted by royal declaration, and is not a creation like the dukedoms. There have been seven princesses royal to date:

1. Princess Mary, daughter of Charles I (date of declaration unknown)
2. Princess Anne, daughter of George II (1727)
3. Princess Charlotte, daughter of George III, the future Queen of Württemberg (1789)
4. Princess Victoria, daughter of Queen Victoria, who later became the German Empress Frederick (1841)
5. Princess Louise, Duchess of Fife, daughter of King Edward VII (1905)
6. Princess Mary, Countess of Harewood, daughter of King George V (1932)
7. Princess Anne, daughter of Queen Elizabeth II (1987)

The Princess Royal with her mother, HM Queen Elizabeth II, at Sandringham on Christmas Day.

Princes of Wales

Welsh Princes AD 844–1282

Rhodri 'The Great'	844–78
Anarawd (son of Rhodri)	878–916
Idwal Foel	916–42
Hywel Dda 'The Good'	942–50
Iago ab Idwal (or Ieuaf)	950–69
Iago	969–79
Hywel ap Ieuaf 'The Bad'	979–85
Cadwallon ap Ieuaf	985–6
Maredudd ab Owain ap Hywel Dda	986–99
Cynan ap Hywel ab Ieauf	999–1008
Llywelyn ap Seisyll	999–1023
Rhyderch ab Iestyn	1023–33
Iago ab Idwal ap Meurig	1033–39
Gruffydd ap Llywelyn ap Seisyll	1039–63
Bleddyn ap Cynfyn	1063–75
Trahaearn ap Caradog	1075–81
Gruffydd ap Cynan ab Iago	1081–1137
Owain Gwynedd	1137–70
Iorwerth Drwyndwn	1170–74
Daffydd ap Owain Gwynedd	1174–94
Llywelyn Fawr 'The Great'	1194–1240
Dafydd ap Llywelyn	1240–46
Llywelyn ap Gruffydd ap Llywelyn (Llewelyn the last)	1267–82

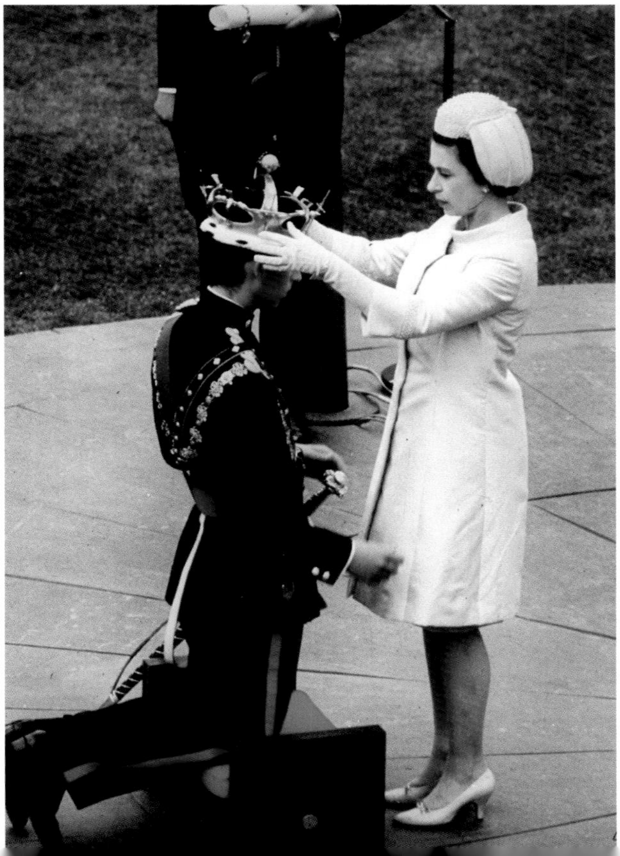

English Princes After AD 1301

Dates of declaration are shown in the right-hand column.

Edward (son of Edward I)	1301
Edward The Black Prince (son of Edward III)	1343
Richard (later Richard II)	1376
Henry of Monmouth (later Henry V)	1399
Edward of Westminster (son of Henry VI)	1454
Edward of Westminster (later Edward V)	1472
Edward (son of Richard III)	1483
Arthur Tudor (son of Henry VII)	1489
Henry Tudor (later Henry VIII)	1504
Henry Stuart (son of James I)	1610
Charles Stuart (later Charles I)	1616
Charles Stuart (later Charles II)	1630
James Francis Edward 'The Old Pretender'	1688
George Augustus (later George II)	1714
Frederick (son of George II)	1729
George William Frederick (later George III)	1751
George Augustus Frederick (later George IV)	1762
Albert Edward (later Edward VII)	1841
George (later George V)	1901
Edward (later Edward VIII)	1910
Charles (son of Queen Elizabeth II)	1958 (invested 1969)

On 1 July 1969 Prince Charles was formally invested as Prince of Wales by his mother Her Majesty The Queen. The ceremony, a scene of eye-catching pageantry, was held at Caernarvon Castle.

Present Royal Line of Succession

The present order of succession to the crown is as follows:

1 HRH The Prince of Wales, KG (Heir Apparent)
2 HRH Prince William of Wales
3 HRH Prince Henry of Wales
4 HRH The Duke of York, KG
5 HRH Princess Beatrice of York
6 HRH Princess Eugenie of York
7 HRH The Earl of Wessex, KG
8 James, Viscount Severn
9 Lady Louise Windsor
10 HRH The Princess Royal, KG
11 Mr Peter Phillips
12 Miss Zara Phillips
13 Viscount Linley
14 Hon. Charles Armstrong-Jones
15 Hon. Margarita Armstrong-Jones
16 Lady Sarah Chatto
17 Samuel Chatto
18 Arthur Chatto
19 HRH The Duke of Gloucester, KG
20 The Earl of Ulster
21 Lord Culloden
22 Lady Davina Lewis
23 Lady Rose Windsor
24 HRH The Duke of Kent, KG
25 Lady Marina Windsor
26 Lady Amelia Windsor
27 Lady Helen Taylor
28 Columbus Taylor
29 Cassius Taylor
30 Eloise Taylor
31 Estella Taylor
32 Lord Frederick Windsor
33 Lady Gabriella Windsor
34 HRH Princess Alexandra, The Hon. Lady Ogilvy, KG
35 Mr James Ogilvy
36 Alexander Ogilvy
37 Flora Ogilvy
38 Mrs Marina Ogilvy
39 Christian Mowatt
40 Zenouska Mowatt

Beyond this point, there are a great number of Lascelles descendants, the issue of the Earl of Harewood (b.1923), and his late brother, Hon. Gerald Lascelles (1924–98), not all of whom are in line. After the descendants of King George V, it is necessary to turn to the descendants of the daughters of King Edward VII: the Duke of Fife and his family, the King of Norway and his children, and then his sisters and their descendants.

After the Norwegian royal family, the line continues with the descendants of Queen Victoria's second son, Alfred, Duke of Edinburgh (also Duke of Coburg), only a few of whom are shown on the tree of the family of Queen Victoria, followed by the descendants of her third son, Arthur, Duke of Connaught, and her youngest son, Leopold, Duke of Albany. After them, the crown would pass to the eligible descendants of Queen Victoria's daughters in order of birth.

Those members of the Royal Family who are Roman Catholics, or married to Roman Catholics, are not in the line of succession.